Tim Niemier

The Millionaire Beach Bum

How I turned my A.D.D. into passion and profit!

I would like to dedicate this book to all the people who cared enough to steer me in the right direction at the right time: This safety net saved me many times and probably kept me from getting saved just as many times. This is also for anyone who has mentored anyone, however big or small, and to anyone who will find time to do this in the future. Sometimes it is to a total stranger but that one gesture could, and I am sure has, altered the course of someone's life.

The human race can either flourish or stumble depending on if we can pass on what we know to the next generation. The value of the second oldest profession, motherhood is underrated. The value of men as mentors in this process is just as important

ONE

THE LETTER

"Life is a game, the object of which is to discover the object."

I nervously opened the letter we had been expecting. It read blah-blah-blah-blah, we will give you blah-blah millions of dollars for your company, Ocean Kayak blah-blah-blah. My wife Rebecca and I looked at each other and read it over again and again. There had to be a catch. The next day we checked it out, and yes, it was a real offer of millions for our company. My world suddenly changed. Ocean Kayak was my whole universe outside my immediate family. Now, someone wanted to buy my life's work? Was this a blessing or a curse? Was I prepared for what would happen next? I was excited and scared at the same time.

A Decade of Sacrifice

The previous decade, Rebecca and I had put ourselves through more than we ever thought possible. Growing a company is like starting a family. We also had a son and daughter during this time. Both our business and our children grew at an incredible rate. Ocean Kayak expanded at an astonishing 30% average per year. Personally, I pushed myself to accomplish goals that I never thought possible. The company was a beautiful obsession. If getting kayakers into the ocean had not been an activity that I truly loved, I would have dropped out of the 10-year marathon much earlier. I had been making kayaks since 1965, but not at this level of production.

The incredible growth of Ocean Kayak had created many stresses on every part of my life. I was working endless hours. Rebecca and I also had a challenge at home, bringing up two very energetic kids. It was a demanding period, but also a very exciting period in my life. I was realizing my dream of turning people on to the water using shapes that I sculpted with my own hands. But sometimes I had to wonder, what is driving me to do all this? I had never worked this hard before on anything.

While My Business Rocketed to Success, My Marriage Crashed

Creating and selling this exciting business could be most people's ultimate dream accomplishment. The previous decade of obsession and hard work plus the stress of selling the business caused our marriage to fall apart. Why did all of this happen at the same time? I wanted to work out my marriage problems, but I didn't know how. I felt this moment was simultaneously my biggest failure and my biggest success.

Rebecca and I had been struggling with our marriage for some time. But as well as being husband and wife, and father and mother to our kids at home, we were business partners. To make it even more complicated, Rebecca's family was involved in the business as well. Rebecca and I knew that if we fought at work, the company wouldn't survive. The business would be worth nothing.

Everything looked great from the outside. Boat sales at Ocean Kayak were fantastic. But we knew that we couldn't continue like we had before. We no longer had the passion or the energy for the business or for each other. But we couldn't just get divorced without affecting our bank loans and the sale of the company. Selling was our only practical option.

Finding the Exit Strategy

In business, the term "exit strategy" is another way of saying, "selling the company." If you don't have an exit strategy for yourself and your company, the guy upstairs does. No one makes it out of this world alive. Selling, or passing on your company, and dying are not events that we may want to look forward to, but they are inevitable. With the letter, we had our exit strategy. Was selling Ocean Kayak selling out, or was the money the ultimate reward? I wasn't sure. But I was fairly certain this was the time to sell the company, before my ultimate exit from all the stress the business had brought to my life.

My Life-Changing Events

My thoughts raced back to my boyhood. When I was less than ten years old, another event both scared me and changed my life. It was the first time I paddled into the deep ocean. We lived in rural (yes, rural) Malibu in the 1950s, when land was cheap because no one wanted to live there. The area was rustic when we moved in. Coyotes and desert tortoises were common. There weren't many kids where I lived. But I grew and matured with Malibu. There I found lifelong friends and I found a lifelong love for the Malibu way of life. When I was growing up, I was afraid of the ocean. Our house had a wide view of the water, and the sea never seemed friendly to me. What was out there? What lurked under the inky blue water? What would happen if I couldn't see the ocean floor?

But my world changed when I paddled a friend's $20 mail-order-kit kayak out through the waves for the first time. From the water's surface, I looked up and saw the house I lived in. I was both scared and excited. Up to that point, I had been an observer of life. This was the most intense experience I had ever had. From that moment, I have been in love with that body of water. The ocean changed me into a participant in life. From the first time I paddled that kayak through the surf, my love affair with the ocean was on an irreversible course with no apparent exit strategy. That was the day the ocean stole my soul.

Spreading the Joy

I soon realized that others could have the same incredible life-transforming experience on the water that I first had. In the Sixties there were virtually no kayaks of any kind or even canoes sold in the whole Los Angeles area. I am proud of having started that whole water friendly, sit-on-top kayak trend, and I'm even more proud of the joy my boats have brought to other people. When I took people out through the surf in Malibu, it was as if they had traveled through a time warp to a different planet. The beach crowds and the busy Pacific Coast Highway suddenly vanished. When the water was clear and the sand and kelp on the bottom were visible, we would feel like we were flying. Sometimes fish darted beneath us; sometimes city bus-sized whales spouted close to us.

Fascination replaced fear. That's why I began to design all sorts of watercraft, each one for a different experience on the water. The ocean has many different moods and conditions. There were magic moments every time I went out alone or with a new paddler. Many people associated these spiritual experiences with the boats I designed. It was really the awe-inspiring ocean that gave them mystical feelings, but I provided the vehicles to get them there.

Overcoming Fear of Water and of Life

The first time I took my own canvas and wood home-built kayak out beyond the surf, I was afraid as I paddled into that foreign space just beyond the surf line. I still experience a bit of fear when I think of my ultimate exit, the one where my body exits this planet. Now that I've lived for many decades, I naturally think about what I would like to have people say about me at my own funeral. What has my life amounted to? I hope the sum total of my eulogy will not be, "He sold his company for millions of dollars". The  second time I paddled out into the ocean in my kayak, I had a little less fear. I loved the feeling of overcoming this fear of the unknown. Eventually, I shared this with other people who were not unlike me; people who were fearful at first but later told me that the experience changed their lives. I call the experience being "water friendly," or maybe even starting a love affair with the water.

What Did the Letter Mean to Me?

So, now there I was with this astounding offer in front of me. I had feelings of joy and accomplishment mixed with anxiety that I would never be the same again. Was this going to be like Faust who sells his soul to the Devil? Would I be forced into some sort of void where I would never have this love affair again? I was experiencing feelings of joy and loss simultaneously. I worried about abandoning my employees. I feared not only the loss of my marriage and Rebecca, but also the loss of her wonderful family. They were a big part of my life. I was afraid, well actually terrified, but knew I had to move ahead. What would happen next in my life, as I knew it?

ReflectionsHunters vs. Farmers

In this book I refer to ADHD and ADD as just ADD to keep things simple. Thom Hartman, the author, talks about the ADD mind being like that of a restless hunter, as contrasted with the non-ADD mind being more like the patient farmer. The farmer likes stability and no surprises or irregularities. The hunter personality is completely different. Hunters are like cats that sit around for hours and appear lazy, but then notice something that indicates prey, when nobody else around has those acute senses or that curiosity. When the goal or the prey is recognized, the hunter is totally on the chase mode, with an intensity of concentration that the farmer may never have.

Recently, there have been discoveries in our genome that suggest that there is a hunter gene that produces different brain chemistry that results in this different behavior. Our evolutionary past suggests that this get-up-and-go behavior gave us a huge advantage when times were tough. This genetic variation helps creative people invent things that are truly novel. My novel idea was simply to make a kayak that one could sit on rather than in. Writing this book helped me fully understand my own life. In each chapter, I will describe a bit of my journey, and then at the end of the chapter, using the miracle of hindsight, I will reflect on what those events meant to me: where I made the right decisions and where I made errors. I thank you for coming along with me on this journey.

TWO

GROWING UP IN MALIBU: MEMORIES OF THE FIFTIES AND SIXTIES

"Old people know more about being young than young people know about being old."

My earliest memories go back to age four or five. We lived in a rented house that was the fourth or fifth house up the hill from the Pacific Coast Highway on Topanga Canyon Boulevard, just north of Los Angeles. The highway went along the edge of the mountains that started to get very steep just north of Topanga. Malibu officially started just west of

Topanga. The coastline there faced due south, so the highway went east and west. We only lived in one of the cheap little rental houses for a year or so. Two miles up the coast and further up the hill, my family was building our dream house.

Our house in Topanga looked out over a creek that meandered down toward the ocean. In that day, our parents let us roam miles from home, even though we were between five and ten years old. I know now that there were just as many creeps back then, but the media hadn't yet broadcast that news to the world, so we lived in blissful ignorance. We also knew which things to avoid.

Exploring the beach was always interesting and the creek formed a nice little surf break that wasn't as good or classic as the point break at the famous Malibu surf spot where the Malibu Creek forms a surf break from left to right. A break like this with the right size waves enables surfers to ride the break sideways, sometimes all the way under the pier, which is almost a quarter mile long ride. This is a "right" point break. At the time, Topanga had nice little waves and was a more private sort of place, whereas Malibu was a public scene.

Life is a Beach

Topanga Beach at that time consisted of a bunch of cheap houses on leased land owned by the Los Angeles Athletic Club. It started along the coast at the mouth of Topanga Creek, where Topanga Canyon Boulevard stretched from the Pacific Coast Highway back into the Santa Monica Mountains. Like many places that are now trendy and expensive, Topanga Beach had its beginnings as a low rent district, but it was an incubator for a whole new way of living.

What made it special was, of course, the ocean. The surf was always changing; it was like having a natural and perpetual roller coaster; free entertainment that was always available, right next to a wonderful beach that was perfect for hanging out with friends and family. The rise and fall of tides, the size and shape of the waves, the light of day and weather altered slowly and continuously, like an ever-changing impressionistic painting. This amazing scene was always right in front of us. The weather was typically good year round; it wasn't even especially hot in the summer. A lot of time there was fog in the morning that burned off at noon and might come back the next morning. Kids could spend the day on the beach while the adults talked and enjoyed the scenery. Many anthropologists believe that when we were just becoming humans, we spent a lot of time on beaches in Africa to survive. That may be why it feels so familiar to us. Maybe the people on the Southern California beaches were reliving that part of our primordial past. Whatever the reason, it just felt good to be there.

The residents came from all over the United States, seeking a new life. A new culture was forming around the beach. Looking out on the water, you could forget that you were a half an hour from the busy town of Santa Monica.

Hanging in Topanga with the Hope Family

Our house in Topanga was about a quarter mile up the canyon. The Hope family lived next door. Their daughter, Patty Hope, was my age. Their son, Bob, was my brother's age. Both Patty and Bob were born in England, but arrived in the U.S. when they were pretty young. Their parents, Harry and Margaret, sometimes told horrible stories about World War II, which was probably the reason they left England to live in California.

Patty and I would walk miles down to Topanga Lane and the creek. The area was very wild in those days. The creek flooded occasionally and wiped out the houses alongside it. Residents had horses and goats. Hanging out at the Hope's house was interesting and different for me. There was a kids' part of the house at the kitchen end; at the other end was a sort of adult part of the house that always seemed to be dimly lit.

Two crossed swords decorated one end of the adult living room and a TV set was centered at the other. On the coffee table was always a stack of magazines with some Playboy magazines at the bottom of the pile. Patty's dad, Harry, in his home workshop, fixed the early television sets with tubes in them; her mom made me tea. Those are my first beautiful memories. I can still taste Margaret's tea and pancakes. I still visited there often, even after my family moved to our new house two miles north.

The Beat Generation

In the 1950s, Malibu was home to the "Beat" generation. The Beatniks and famous beat poets mobbed a popular coffeehouse between Big Rock, where we lived, and Topanga, two miles away. The parking area was filled with cars on weekends. Folk music and coffeehouses were on the cutting edge of change. No cold or snow in the winter was another big plus. California was being discovered. People streamed out from the rest of the United States, attracted to the mild winters. Folk music was an alternative to the popular Elvis-type rock and roll; many felt that folk music was a more emotional expression. There was a distinct middle class in Malibu; snobby behavior was not "in."

My Parents' Dream House

I think that my parents dreamed of a house and a life that would be a safe place in the world of struggle they

were born

into. My mother and father were both born in 1914. They were teens when the Great Depression hit in 1930. After America emerged from that decade of despair, my parents were just old

enough to go through the Second World War. Their dream house was like a piece of artwork. Facing south, its huge glass windows encompassed a 180-degree view of the Pacific Ocean,

including Catalina Island. It was only the second or third house completed on a very steep hillside above Malibu. Each weekend, as Malibu got busier and more people moved to the coast from the

valleys, we would hear honking and sirens on the highway out of sight below us. Sometimes the traffic jams on Sunday afternoon from the returning beachgoers would be 10 miles long. We were glad we could stay above all the racket and crowds below.

My Parents: Creative and Hands-On

My father had taken flying lessons in 1936 and wanted to fly for England and the RAF in Europe. Most of those pilots never made it back. My dad actually went to Canada to try to enlist in the RAF, but his father convinced him to return and join the U.S. Military. He served as a crew

chief and airplane mechanic in the South Pacific, where he seemed to get shot at a lot, despite not being on the front lines of the infantry. He

sustained a knee injury and ended up in a Santa Monica hospital, where he met my mother and got married in 1945, ready to start a new life. Both my mother and father were formally

trained in Art. My father worked in aerospace doing graphic design.

My mother was born in Saskatchewan, Canada, but moved to Michigan, where her parents were from originally. Her father died at the end of the swine flu epidemic in 1918. Her relatives had been in the States since the 1700s, descendant from English and Scottish ancestors. Her maiden name was Mitchel. Around the time my mother and father met, the first full-length animated movie had just come out. Fantasia came out from Disney. My mother worked on the animation in that movie. I still have some of her artwork from that project.

My mother became a dedicated teacher who inspired many of her students to follow their passions and develop a fascination for what drove them, rather than just settling for good scores on tests. I was aware of this because parents of her students would often tell her that her teaching influence had been a turning point in their child's life. My father grew up in South Bend, Indiana, the descendent of two Niemier cousins who came to America from the German/Prussia/Poland area in the mid-1800s. Just about all the American Niemiers I have run into seem to have roots in South Bend. There are only a few thousand Niemiers now living east of Berlin and in Poland. In talking to relatives, I have discovered that there is a tradition of craftsmanship that runs deep in the family. I know little about what my descendants did before they came over to America, other than that it was noted somewhere that they were machinists. My dad followed the tradition; he was always building something. He had put himself through art school and later ran his own commercial art business in Santa Monica. There are still some signs in the area that I recognize as his work.

Trial by Fire in Malibu

Around 1957, we moved into the dream house. The local wildlife, mountain lions, turtles, lizards, foxes and other animals hadn't quite moved out yet. Before we  were completely moved in a fire burned all the hillsides. My dad managed to put out the fire around our house and even saved the house next door from burning. Every decade or so in that time period, Malibu had a fire that traveled 20 to 50 miles an hour pushed by the powerful Santa Ana winds that could blow over 60 miles an hour offshore. The fires usually lasted less than a week and evacuated residents didn't know if they'd come home to a blackened foundation or an untouched house. But fires were just part of life in Malibu.

My Family Life: Not Always a Happy Home

For me, family life was pretty rough. My brother, who went to a Catholic School, was four years older, and definitely had an attitude. In the neighborhood, he was just known as "the Niemier boy." He took out much of his anger on me with threats and physical abuse and my parents ignored his behavior or weren't equipped to deal with it. I now think he was trying to find his limits and my parents were attempting to take a more "modern" laissez-faire approach regarding physical punishment.

THREE

GRADE SCHOOL YEARS: 1957-63

"Education is what you get from reading the fine print. Experience is what you get from not reading it."

I remember having a fairly pleasant experience at Webster Elementary School. It seemed like the teachers enjoyed their jobs. I also remember the playground pavement being so rough that, when you fell on it, you would go back to check how much flesh was left on the ground. Years later, at a high school reunion, when I sat down at a table of classmates from Malibu, I realized I had gone to grade school with all of them. We were all born in California and witnessed the invasion of people who moved in from everywhere. We posted our old pictures on a Facebook page. It's amazing how the past can bring perspective, isn't it? We are all so incredibly self-centered as children. At that reunion, I learned about so many things I was unaware of while growing up.

At home, both my parents were active with their hands. My father was always busy making or fixing things around the house. He made models of sailing ships; I still have a rowboat he created. I put some of them in the bath; now I feel guilty because they weren't completely waterproof.

My mother mixed coffee grounds with paraffin and old crayon ends for specks of color and poured the mixture into milk cartons. When these wax blocks cooled, I carved them with a dull knife into tikis and animal images. Eventually I started using chisels and carving wood to make sculptures. Early in life, I learned to transform one thing into another; I especially loved to carve things I could hold in my hand.

Finding My Best Buddy, Dan DeVault

While I was in grade school, the neighborhood grew. With more houses on our steep hill, there were more kids to play with. When people finally moved into the only house close to ours, I walked over and asked, "Do you have any kids my age?" There were two: Dorrie, my age, and Dan, a bit younger than myself. At my young age, I could relate to the boys better, so for years Dan and I created our own adventures with kayaks, bicycles, backpacking, and, later, expeditions to Canada. As boys, we could eat at either household. We would see who had the most attractive prospects for dinner and then eat at the appropriate house

At the time, most white folks had not yet discovered jazz. However, the album Take Five was often playing next door at the DeVault's house, because Dan's father was very much into jazz. He had

albums, not only from Dave Brubeck, but also from many of the great black musicians. Many frequented the old jazz places along the waterfront communities a few miles south of Malibu, closer to Los Angeles. The Nichols family lived in another house up the hill. It was a great place to go because the Nichols had all sorts of hobbies going on. I have a lot of great memories of building things. We kids designed and built balsa wood gliders. Johnny Nichols was a year older than I was and his brother Rusty was my brother's age. This family actively played 1950s and 1960s folk music, such as Peter, Paul and Mary, which included a lot of messages about civil rights.

Junior High School Years - 1963 to 1966

At grammar school graduation, we had a special brunch with little surfboards on our placemats. Someone wrote predictions of what we would all be doing when we grew up. I was supposed to become some sort of designer, maybe for cars.

The next year, we became the first grade at the new Malibu Park Junior High School; located at the north end of Malibu, above Zuma Beach This was fifteen miles away by an uncomfortable bus ride. We lived a mile up the hill, which involved carpooling or just walking. In the summer the rattlesnakes liked to lie on the warm pavement in the morning, but we knew to watch for them, so they weren't a problem. The good part was that we ended up being the top class for all three years. There were only about one hundred students and most of the teachers were young and wanted to change the world. My math teacher, Mr. Newcomb, would read science fiction books to teach us that there was more to math than numbers. He understood that imagination is more important than knowledge.

The Start of My Art

The school held a contest to design the cover of the school annual. Our mascot was the Spartan, so I drew a Spartan warrior on a horse with a sword and won the contest. Winning really meant a lot to me, because I didn't fit in and I didn't feel like I was succeeding in school. My grades weren't bad, but they weren't outstanding, either. In some classes (such as honors classes) I would do well; in others, I really struggled.

I was depressed and lonely. I started to figure out things in my head and to imagine things and pictures of things all in my head, in class or anywhere. I thought in terms of pictures, not words. I struggled a lot with school and didn't know why. I was inside myself. Talking with girls seemed to be impossible as though

SPARTANS '65

we spoke two completely different languages. I liked band class, because the music seemed to sink into my brain.

In physical education class, sometimes I would just let everything go and run all out on the last lap, because it felt so good. I also liked to work out on the bars and had the school record for twenty-nine chin-ups. I will always remember that when President Kennedy was shot, the principal announced it during break, when I was half finished with an ice cream bar.

At home, I focused on my art. I carved more often and I tried to refine small shapes. One of the most ambitious was a representation of Gershwin's Rhapsody in Blue, where I attempted to carve into special shapes what the notes sounded like to me. Another carving was of a squirrel where I carved a stylized tail that came up over the top of the animal. Later I realized that this shape became the same swoop of many of the kayaks I designed, because it also fit the form the water made as a kayak glided through it. Overall, I was confused with growing up.

Shop Class Transforms My Brother

My brother finally made it into Santa Monica High School and found his passion: the shop class. Our garage occasionally had a car in it, but most of the time we used it as a busy workshop. When we set up the garage, my brother wanted to arrange it just like the shop class, where one whole wall was plywood with little pegs to hold the tools, so that at a glance you can see if any tool is missing. Shop class for my brother was the only thing he could relate to in school; it really changed his life. He started modifying every mechanical device in sight. Even the lawn mower got a new custom ground high lift cam with a stronger valve spring and straight exhaust with higher gearing. It would go 15 miles an hour and cut through the thickest grass. In his bedroom, my brother would tape cutout magazine pictures of hot rods and motorcycles over the entire wall space. Sometimes I would go in and look at them all. Despite the abuse I took from him, we were still brothers and I still thought he had some cool stuff.

My brother and I started to buy motorcycles and rebuild them. I took the frame and other parts of my brother's old Triumph 650 cc motorcycle to Malibu Park to sandblast

them; and I thought it was cool to show off the motorcycle stuff on the school bus. I enjoyed riding the motorcycles more than the rebuilding work, but my brother was the exact opposite; he loved maintaining them. I modified a special one myself. It was a bike from Czechoslovakia called a Jawa. But the engine had quit running and I couldn't get parts. I found a modified but very reliable Honda engine bored out to 337 cc. The result was a superior motor in a better handling motorcycle.

FOUR

MOTORCYCLES AND BICYCLES TRANSFORM ME

"Ahh I am finally mobile and I can finally fly away"

Malibu has always consisted of a few housing clusters surrounded by vast wide-open mountains with a few dirt roads. I rode motorcycles all over the surrounding hills. At the end of the road we lived on was a large flat area. I made a track there and rode around and around on it. At age 13 to 15, I didn't have a driver's license yet, so I also started getting into ten-speed bicycles that I would buy cheap and rebuild. Then I would ride them farther and farther away from home. I rode 15 miles to the Junior High School in 45 minutes. When my brother was at his worst, the bicycle was my ticket out of the scene at my house. It was my escape.

Another friend, Don Dryer, liked to race bicycles. Don was my age, his brother John was my brother's age, and we all had motorcycles. John actually raced on a track and had an Italian Parrella 250 that was pretty fast. John worked at a motorcycle shop in town, Jack Baldwin Motorcycles. I saw Mel Torme and other celebrities there. John would say that the owner sponsored him with free parts. There was only one sticky detail about that sponsorship: Jack Baldwin didn't know about it.

The Dryers had no horses but a horse corral came with their house, so inside that they built an oval track with a few jumps. Every Friday they had races complete with cheerleaders and mini-grandstands. They had qualifier races, semi-main and main event races just like the regular motorcycle races. We even welded up bikes with sidecars and raced them. But all this fun came to a halt when the Dryer's insurance agent told them that someone might hurt themselves and sue them.

Toward the end of the Dryer speedway era, I welded English road bike pedals and bearings with a longer pedal arm together in a Schwinn American bike frame and put a Stingray banana seat on it, with suspension in the seat posts that went to the rear axle. The bike slid on fast downhill dirt roads and handled just like a flat track motorcycle.

One day in Junior High, as I was walking by the bus shed, I spotted pieces of a motorcycle in a box. It was a 1952 BSA 650 twin with an A10 motor, with two plungers for rear suspension and no swing arm. The bike was one year younger than I was. A bus driver owned it. I asked if it was for sale and ended up buying the whole project for $25.

It was my last year in Junior High School. I spent all year working on that motorcycle so it would be ready for my first year at Santa Monica High School. I had the biggest bike there, though not the fastest. I was hooked on riding on bikes of any kind. To me, two spinning wheels represented total freedom.

Getting into Kayaks

It was also around this time that I noticed Dan DeVault, from next door, had bought a kayak in a kit. The frame consisted of only four long wood poles about one inch by one inch and a few other little pieces to spread them apart. All four poles came together at a point at either end. Regular duck canvas covered the whole thing, sealed on the outside with Sears Navajo White latex house paint, and applied by Dan's sister, Dorrie. Dan had spent an equal amount of money to buy a paddle.

When the paint dried, we decided to put the kayak in the ocean. The water looked so tame from up on the hillside where we lived. But when we carried it to water's edge, the surf seemed much bigger. We took turns in the boat and somehow made it out through the surf, even though the top of the kayak was completely open. For me, emerging into the swells from the surf was like going through a magic portal into another world. All of a sudden, everything changed. The world abruptly became quiet. I was just being there, truly in the moment. I was a little frightened, because the thin canvas covering was the only barrier between me and the deep and mysterious blue sea. I couldn't help wondering what was swimming beneath me. When we finally got home and I looked down at the ocean from my house, my world had changed. The ocean had stolen my soul.

Adventures by Kayak

After we took Dan's simple mail order kayak out in the ocean, I wanted to design a longer, sleeker one with better lines. I made drawings and laid out the project on paper, trying to imagine how much volume I would need to make this shape both fast and stable. Years later, when I pulled out those drawings; I saw they were remarkably close to the patterns I created for Ocean Kayak's designs. My first kayak was also painted canvas on a wood frame, but different from Dan's mail order boat in that mine had a vertical slicing bow, instead of a pointed bow like a whitewater boat. I also added more stringers to make a stronger craft. I built a double bladed paddle like Dan's to go with it.

After I finished building my kayak, Dan and I took our boats out at the same time. This was another great first-time experience because we could finally both go out into the ocean together. Mine proved to be faster and tracked straighter, while Dan's tended to waggle more, but both got us out on the water. It was still a hassle to get my mom to take us up and down the hill in the old station wagon. One time, while I was still in junior high school with no driver's license, I decided to do a big trip up the coast. I had my mother take the kayak in the back of the station wagon down to the shore, and then I started paddling north. The trip was a lot farther than I had ever gone before. (There is only one way to find one's limits.) I was joined by a pod of grey whales swimming right next to me. They were not threatening but definitely got my attention. When I turned the corner, there was a long sandy beach called Zuma Beach, named after a native chief from the area. I pulled in and carried my kayak to the nearest phone booth, and called mom who picked me up. Mission accomplished. The experience was a bit frightening, but I couldn't wait to do it all over again. The problem with my first kayak was that it was a hassle to get though the surf. I was used to body surfing and diving through the waves. I didn't want to be separated from the ocean; I wanted to be part of it.

Why Didn't I Surf Like Everyone Else?

The surf culture was growing strong; it seemed like everyone wanted to do it. But whenever I saw I lot of people doing the same thing, I wanted to do something different. (I'm still the same way now.) There were some classic surfboard makers in the area that had shops on the street. Con Surfboards was just a few blocks from the water on 2nd or 3rd Street near Pico, and Dave Sweet's shop was up Olympic Boulevard. Sweet was one of the first people to use foam for the body of the surfboard and then fiberglass a hard surface over the lightweight core. Those boards were beautiful, but I wanted to create something of my own. I was a non-conformist.

FIVE

THE TIMES, THEY WERE A-CHANGING

"It feels a lot more to me like I did when I got here, than I do right now"

By the Sixties, the culture was changing in Malibu. The Beat Generation was about to switch into the Hippie Generation. Drugs were starting to show up. LSD was legal; it was considered a great anti-depressant drug. My friend's father was part of a government study to determine if LSD was effective. He was sorry to see it become illegal. Of course, he took much less LSD than many people took to go on acid trips; the quantity

33

changes the entire nature of the effect. Marijuana, or pot, was the drug of the times because a joint was portable and easily shared. This was a major generational difference between pot and alcohol, which was not shared. Everything was changing.

My brother graduated from Santa Monica High School in 1965. I started high school in 1966 and graduated in 1969, so we were never in the same school at the same time. The pictures in our school yearbooks were as different as night and day. Guys' hair went from 1965 neat and tidy to 1969 long and wild. Topanga Canyon was Hippie Central. The canyon became the place to live. Someone even rented out their doghouse. The era was insane. I loved the ideals of the time, but not the insistence on non-conforming, which was, of course, conforming all over again.

On to Santa Monica High School

On one of the first days of school at Santa Monica High, all the girls had to have their skirts measured to be sure no hems were more than a few inches above their knees. Some girls were sent home. I started football and marching band a few weeks before the school year began. I wanted to do everything. The first year I was not on the varsity team, but I made the B team, which had a great lineup. We won all but one game. I liked football because it was impossible to fake your performance. You did what you had to do or you looked like an idiot. I played Guard right next to the Center, so there was a lot of contact.A few other guys were in both football and the band. I played snare drums and got a kick out of beating the rhythm to keep everyone in step even when the band wasn't playing. I enjoyed all of that. My classes, however, were often disappointing. There was a great English class called Western World Ideas that taught about Carl Jung's archetypes. You could identify the brainy students on sight, because they wore slide rules in holsters on their belts. (This was before pocket calculators.) Art classes turned me off because they were mostly drawing. The little sculpture we did was lame and certainly didn't involve carving wood or making kayaks. There were, however, pretty good shop classes both in junior high and high school.

Depression

In my senior year in High School I was going to be in the Varsity Football team and be in the marching band as well. At the beginning of that final season, I slammed my head somehow  during football practice and got a concussion. This is where the brain actually gets bruised which can cause severe problems later in life. As a result I felt really withdrawn and suffered depression. Part of it was just adjusting to growing up. Some of it was the disillusion I felt after I came back that summer from Outward Bound in Oregon to a place that I expected to be paradise after the hardship of the wilderness and being homesick. When I got home it wasn't as special as I had remembered it. I had enough units from going to summer school so I graduated a semester early and went right into the City College just a few blocks up Pico Blvd in Santa Monica. Even after going to this Community College I still felt out of place and depressed and alienated. It was a confusing time overall, and I hadn't found myself yet.

Into the Wilderness: Backpacking

Dan and I got excited about the solitude of backpacking. Bob Sherman, a neighbor who would later figure prominently in my life, introduced us to the Sierras. In 1968, Dan and I figured backpacking would  never get popular and we'd have the whole place to ourselves. We went farther into the Sierras than Bob had taken us before. Sometimes we borrowed a car from one of the households and did a big loop. Other times we bussed up to the east side, hiked across the Sierras, and then hitchhiked down to the bus station and got a ticket home. Sometimes we would hike up too early in the season and find parts of the trail still snowed in. We carried 1 lb. of food a day per person and worked to keep everything else ultra-light. Our packs weighed only about 32 lbs. for a two-week trip. We would usually fish to supplement our meager diet. Even with the fish, I often lost five to eight lbs. on a trip. Within a few years, the trails got pretty crowded. When we needed a permit to go on trails, Dan suggested we get into kayaking instead, as it would never be that popular.

SIX

A GIANT LEAP FORWARD

"From the Girl Scouts to a fiberglass Sit On Top Kayak in 3 easy lessons"

My career in design took a giant leap forward with Holly Love, who was my "second mom" in the neighborhood. Holly and Charlie Love had a son, Martin, who was my brother's age and a daughter, Janis, who was just a bit older than I was. Charlie built the very first computers. He was a scientist with a goatee beard who drove a little Triumph sports car. Holly drove a Citroen. They were very likable and delightfully different at the same time. Holly would get excited about the new sound of Bob Dylan. She will always be a true friend.

Holly was taking sculpture classes way up Topanga Canyon at Jon Raymond's studio. Wood was the main medium. Jon had a casual way of teaching and the whole class was sort of like a big party and therapy session all in one. I couldn't afford to pay anything but I would go in and clean up and sometimes sand wood sculptures for others. I really liked being around adults more than my peers, perhaps because I hated all the competition in my own age group. I learned a new aesthetic there

that I never got in any public school classroom.

I Join the Girl Scouts

I was never in the Boy Scouts. Instead, I was sort of in the Girl Scouts. It involved canoes. Holly Love's daughter, Janis, was in the Scouts and one of the leaders was Vera Tasker, whose husband Paul

was often present, too. Twice a year the Girl Scouts went down the Colorado River between Blyth and Yuma on the border between Arizona and California, right before the river dives into Mexico. That part of the Colorado is very beautiful, running through dry, sunny country. Usually by day three of a weeklong trip, many of the girls were burnt to a crisp and wore long-sleeved shirts to stay out of the sun. In the spring, the mosquitoes were so bad one day I counted 150 bites on my body. You could see wild horses and other wildlife on the riverbanks, but ten feet in any direction was dry desert. Somehow they figured out that it was good to have a few boys on the trip, maybe to lift the canoes. No matter why, I wasn't complaining. The food was always great and it was fun to be outnumbered by teenage girls. I also liked being in the big 18-foot canoes that were built by the Scout leaders.

Learning from Outward Bound

One Girl Scout on a canoe trip told me about Outward Bound, a wilderness program. The idea fascinated me; I have always been drawn to the wilderness. She talked about the pinnacle of the program, which was a three-day solo where you survived all on your own  and had to forage for your own food and make your own shelter. The Outward Bound program was fabulous. It gave me a completely different view of where I came from.

The Girl Scout Leaders Get Me into Fiberglass

The fiberglass training from the Girl Scout leaders was about to start. At the time, it was almost impossible to buy canoes in the LA area. No one sold them. The Scout leaders were going to build some more canoes. I asked if I could build two for myself. They said, the more the merrier. We ordered the fiberglass cloth and resin and oak gunnels and stainless screws for the trim. The material for each canoe was about $150. We all worked together and put one layer after another on each half of the molds. Then we put the halves together upside down and sealed the bottom by applying about 10 layers of fiberglass, starting with narrow strips first and increasing the width as we moved outward to make a smooth transition from bottom to top of the boat.

Surf de la vieja escuela (1950-60)

We could build one canoe a day, not including the wood gunnels. I originally planned to sell one canoe and keep the other for myself, but I ended up selling both. But most importantly, I learned how to build a fiberglass boat of my own.

Why Not Turn a Tandem Surfboard into a Sit-on-Top Kayak?

I frequently visited Shell's Pawn Shop on 3rd Street in Santa Monica to see what recent treasures they had collected. I saw a huge surfboard made by the Holden Company, designed for tandem surfing. Back then, there were contests where strong guys would pair up with light girls and put them on their  shoulders or perform other stunts while riding the waves. But instead of a tandem surfboard, in front of me I saw my first sit-on-top kayak just waiting to happen. I bought the board for $25 and took it home. At home, I commenced carving out seat and heel depressions, as well as a hatch area where I planned to put dive gear. Dan and I had just started skin diving, holding our breath without tanks. We bought wetsuits for $40 on sale and melted our own lead for weights and we were ready to go. Now we could have a place to put everything. We would load our gear on the board and then I would paddle out while Dan swam out. We started catching lobsters. I thought to myself, how could life get any better than this? After building the canoes with the molds, I figured why not make a mold for a hollow kayak that I could put more dive gear in?

Venturing into Scuba with Kayaks

I reasoned that if we had a hollow kayak similar to the surfboard I adapted, we'd be able to put one tank inside. I created the original design from plaster in our driveway. I made the bow straight up and down to slice through the water instead of riding on top like a surfboard. Then I shaped everything else out. My mom thought this was like a big class art project; she loved it. My dad made me clean up every night. This functional sculpture was really starting excite me.

Carving this first fiberglass mold out of plaster was like doing wood sculpture but bigger. I now understood how to use molds, not only because of building the canoes, but also because around this time I worked with a marble sculptor named Eino, who lived up in the mountains. He was Finnish and his wife was from Germany. I helped him with some of his bronze sculptures that  used lost wax, which taught me about molding. Eino made huge marble chain links and other sculptures that would push the limits of what an artist could do with a material like marble. I also learned about lost wax bronze casting.

For a while I worked at his studio and took care of his farm of goats and other animals while he and family were away getting marble from somewhere or on a trip to Baja. One of the features I remember adding to my molds while I was working up there was the bump that ran lengthwise down the middle of what used to be a flat hull. This middle "bump" formed a great place for the tank to slip into so we could put one inside between the feet and another one forward and even another one in the back. We started out building a kayak to hold one scuba tank and ended up with places for three.

Dan helped me and we built two kayaks. We had to put the two halves together by sticking our heads in the hatches. We had to develop new techniques for sticking the halves together. Working with the fiberglass was messy. Before we discovered gloves, we got it all over ourselves. Grinding fiberglass creates a gritty powder that can make you itch for days, especially if it gets into a nylon sleeping bag. We finally got done with our new kayaks. They worked well because the bows sliced the water but the boats were fairly flat on the bottom and sort of surfed, too. The resulting boats were much longer than surfboards and we could even surf on offshore swells and waves

Reflections

The Lover or Dreamer

Carl Jung talks about the four archetypes that relate to the different parts of the day. The morning is the archetype of the Lover, or what I refer to as the Dreamer. When I relate to this aspect of behavior or feeling, I think of unbounded imagination. I think of waking up from a dreamlike state where I have been flying. Anything is possible and the constraints of daily life haven't set in yet.

The Deep Sea as a Metaphor for the Subconscious Mind

For me, being on a kayak is like floating around on my subconscious mind with all of my fears and feelings somewhere beneath me. Our childhoods are what our conscious selves float on as we go through life. The water is just as dreamlike as our childhood. Instead of embracing the drug scene as an adolescent, I embraced physical activity and took risks, backpacking in the wilderness and exploring the world on bikes, motorcycles, and kayaks. It was a much safer way to rebel than dropping out with LSD and other popular drugs of the time. I still like to prove I'm physically capable of all sorts of activities. I still do forty pushups and twenty pull-ups regularly. My passion for being one with the ocean began when I was a child and I embrace that passion as an adult. What were you passionate about as a child? Did that passion carry over into your adult life? Do you want it to?

SEVEN

I BECOME AN ENTREPRENEUR - 1971 to 1981

"Design and build then ask questions later"

In March of 1971, when I was twenty years old, a guy on the beach said he wanted to buy one of my kayaks. I hadn't done any advertising, but people noticed that I had something on top of my car that wasn't a surfboard, so they tried to figure out what it was. There was and always will be a group of people that want to be on the cutting edge of whatever is happening on the water, and this guy was the first to ask me to sell him one.

I didn't know quite what to say. I made quick calculations in my head before I blurted out a price of $150. The kayak materials cost under $50 in the 1970s and I reasoned that if Dan DeVault and I each made $50, that would be great. In those days, $10 was like $100 of today's dollars, so it seemed like a reasonable amount of money. I didn't want to be greedy. This was my first official sale and for the first time I thought of work I had done as a business. Yahoo!

I was working in construction with Bob Sherman and I was also almost out of the technical school in Santa Monica that we nicknamed Pico Tech, because it was, after all, a technical school on Pico Boulevard. The place was officially called Santa Monica City College, and tuition was a whopping $7.50.

I was still pretty shy, but starting to come out of my shell in the Age of Aquarius. The world was being reinvented. I don't know if it was caused by the concussion or just the confusion of growing up in this era, but I went through a period of depression. I wanted to do something different after high school, so at the college I played off-season water polo with the varsity team. I played informal college soccer. The players spoke Spanish and we didn't have or need a coach. I started swimming a lot and began to feel really well again.

The war in Viet Nam (always two words in the 1970s, but usually combined today) was still raging on. It was tearing the U.S. apart because, unlike today, much of the blood and gore was televised. Vietnamese victims of bombing screamed on the evening news. TV audiences saw anti-war protestors at home getting billy clubbed by the police. There were no illusions about what was going on. One of my motorcycle buddies, Gary Johnson, was a gunner on the same type of Huey helicopter my brother flew. Gary got shot and died there.

My brother convinced me to sign up for the Coast Guard waiting list at age 15. The Coast Guard was a five and a half year commitment but only six months of active duty and the other five years in the reserves. The Seventies were wonderful and crazy all at once.

Freewheeling and Frightening Times

Somewhere in this time period, my brother John changed his name to Jul. He got my job doing construction with Bob Sherman. Bob rode the early English motorcycles and always had something to say about them. In Bob's younger years, he drank hard and lived hard. He was also quite a conservative Republican; he always supported the conservative platform. There was a real rift between the liberal and conservative factions back then, even in our little neighborhood, but somehow we managed to get along.

By spending time with Bob, I learned that I could appreciate certain aspects of a personality without believing in all the same things they did. Bob told my brother to invest the $10,000 he had saved from the military and put it into rental income property. Jul bought his first building and then made about $600 per month. I believe this was one of the best bits of advice my brother ever received. From my parents' point of view, that was probably the one thing my brother was doing right. Jul was trying so hard to catch up that when they looked at me, they simply said, "Just don't be any crazier than your brother and we won't bug you." I decided I would do anything I wanted to do, regardless of whether or not my goals matched the ideals of someone's conservative parents or those of my Hippie generation. I was becoming my own person, and enjoying it.

Looking for My Own Path and the Watermen of the Time

Just off Pico on 4th Street was Con Surfboards. Gary Seaman was there for years until Hoyle Schweitzer had him build the first windsurfer, called the Baja Board. I later hired Gary at Ocean Kayak and he helped me in R&D to make new designs. He was the best of the best and a true master at making the classic surfboards. He worked there many years after I sold the company and made many great contributions. Up Olympic Boulevard at about 20th, I think, there was Dave Sweet Surfboards, the first place that used two-part urethane foam as a core to create the first modern lightweight surfboard. Before that, surfboards were solid wood or hollow plywood paddleboards that weighed a ton. At the time I didn't know Joe Quigg, who built boards in Malibu, but I got to know him well later in Hawaii, on Oahu. Joe surfed but he was also a master at building big sailing catamarans. He was instrumental in the early development of that type of boat.

Paddling Around on Boards

Old style paddleboards that were paddled by hand (not like the standup boards nowadays with a long paddle) had been around way before I made my kayaks. The old surfboards were quite large; the paddleboards were just a little bigger. They were made for paddling, not for surfing as they are today. These paddleboards were also used for racing and skin diving. What people did with paddleboards in that era was amazing. Paddling across from Catalina to the mainland, some 32 miles, for a race was not unusual. I figured out that those boarders would average 5 to 6 miles per hour, which is faster than most sea kayaks of today. Most amazing of all, they didn't use paddles. Some paddlers would lie on their stomachs; others would kneel. The paddleboards and surfboards of the day were so big that my classmates would kneel to catch waves. They did that so much that they would develop giant "surf bumps" on their feet and knees, calluses that were a half-inch thick and more than an inch in diameter. Some surfers escaped the army draft and serving in Viet Nam because the Army boots wouldn't fit their feet.

In San Diego, skin divers would dive off these huge plywood boards that weighed about 100 pounds. After fiberglass construction became more popular, the board builders made hollow paddleboards that were about 20 feet long with a turned-up bow so the kelp didn't get caught on them. In northern California, these were popular with free divers. Most diving was off the beach and with one of these boards a diver could travel a mile or two to get to the good spots.

EIGHT

PADDLEBOARD DIVING

"Life in Classic California on and off the Beach"

One summer Dan DeVault and I got a crazy job driving a car around San Jose with a stopwatch so our bosses could evaluate if one stop signal system was faster than another. The job was only for a few months, so we had prearranged housing. A skin diver lived there in our apartment complex. He invited us to meet his buddies and go diving with them. Skin diving or free diving is different than scuba diving. At this time, everyone and their dog was into scuba diving lessons that would bring lot of cumbersome equipment. Free diving is much more old school, simple and pure. In free diving you hold your breath while underwater instead of sucking air from a scuba tank.

These old school divers were the real deal, holdovers from a bygone do-it-yourself era. They made their own wetsuits by cutting and gluing them together with special wetsuit rubber cement. Their wetsuits didn't include fabric on either side because they claimed the suit would be warmer and allow a diver to swim faster without fabric attached. These special wetsuits would really slip through the water and completely fit the free diving style of descending to 65-foot depths. This was a completely different and independent style of diving than scuba, which instructors taught to large numbers of people and was a real business. Free diving is generally safer than tank diving because there is no need to decompress after being too deep too long. These free divers carried little Styrofoam floats with fishing line and a tiny weight attached. If they were diving for an abalone, and saw a fish, they would put out the weight and Styrofoam to mark the place so they could get back to the same spot. To propel their paddleboards, they would lie on their bellies and use their hands. They also used three-foot-long flippers in a sort of frog kick that moved them along pretty well.

The paddleboard diving tradition had been around for some time, but the early paddleboards were heavy plywood that sometimes leaked. These paddleboards were hollow fiberglass, usually made by a guy who sold them one at a time. The boards were quite long at around 20 feet, pointed at either end with a flat spot for your chest and a large hatch in front of that for spear guns and other gear.

Before the Ocean Kayaks, Dan and I had inflatable surf mats and we would ask the others to carry our weights for us to the dive spot. The water was cold and our suits weren't as warm. To free dive, you breathe extra hard or hyperventilate, while lying perfectly still on the surface of the water. After one last breath, you slip beneath the water and to conserve air, keeping your movements very smooth and as effortless as possible.

Most of the time, the free diving experience is very meditative, but all diving has risks. Once, while diving to 65 feet, I found that I had too much weight on. At about 20  feet down, my suit compressed and I sank very fast. I thought I had plenty of time to get back, but when I turned for the surface, it seemed like I was taking forever to get there. Right before I hit the surface, my vision narrowed and I almost blacked out before I took that first very big breath.

Diving and Surfing at Santa Cruz

We went out at Santa Cruz to get abalone, and then down to Stillwater around Monterey and Carmel to get big ling cod. Dan and I would buy a huge sack of potatoes and onions and have fish or abalone and chips. The hand-and-foot paddling and diving experiences I had while doing the traffic survey job had a major influence later on Ocean Kayak because I thought, why not use a paddle? By sitting up and propelling a board or kayak with a paddle, I could go faster and through larger surf. After developing the Ocean Kayak, we would revisit Santa Cruz but this time on a kayak that was half paddleboard because we sat on top, not inside them like regular kayaks. Our sit-on-top kayaks had the same big hatch as paddleboards, but also had something new, a well for scuba tanks in the back. At only 14 feet long, they would surf on the large waves that would sometimes come in at Steamers Lane surf break. Our kayaks were a lot quicker and easier to move around to the right spot to catch a wave before it got too steep. Using my old Scupper kayaks, we could take off from the outer reef at Steamers Lane and we could ride the same wave all the way into the pier, a long distance. Then we could paddle back out faster to catch the next "set" of large waves.

Diving and Fishing from Kayaks

The Ocean Kayaks continued to evolve so they could hold more and more gear. We started scuba diving with tanks because we were doing deeper dives at the edge of the Malibu kelp beds where the abalone and lobsters were. Having three tanks and a weight belt aboard made the kayak pretty heavy but once it was moving it seemed to cut through the surf like a half-submerged submarine rather than rising up and over each wave. We could get out to the edge of the kelp in Malibu in just a few minutes carrying our tanks, and then spend an hour or two under water in places that were hard to free dive.

One time after I had just paddled in, another diver on the beach asked to try out my kayak. He could not believe that he could get himself all the way out past the surf and to the edge of the kelp in less than five minutes. This feat would normally take him at least half an hour to swim and half the air from his tank. In comparison, I carried three tanks ready and lunch.

The Power of a Father's Words

My dad suggested that I get into real estate like my brother, rather than try to make a living from kayaks, an idea which appeared to be a real long shot. At the time there were probably only half a

55

dozen stores that even carried canoes, let alone kayaks, in the entire L.A. area. I did not want to be like my brother. I vowed to make my kayak business a success. I didn't realize how much this simple statement would affect my future.

A Passion for Transforming Everything, Including My Car

I drove motorcycles until I was about 19, then sold the bike and got a 1959 Volkswagen Beetle. Of course I couldn't drive an ordinary Beetle. Instead, I put a plywood pickup bed on it to make it easier to

Niemier Trucking Co. – 1971

haul dive gear and construction materials. I could also sleep back there, because, in back of the seats the rear window folded down so my feet were about where the steering wheel was. Later I fashioned a camper with a pop-top that I could sit upright in. I painted the whole thing green.

My father had taken early retirement at 55 years old. We did body work in our driveway and called our business Malibu Auto Body. We did body work on my dad's antique restorations and worked on cars for the money. We painted them outdoors; no one cared because Malibu was not a city and had no regulations about such a business. I look back on this time as a very enjoyable sharing experience we had together.

During afternoon tea, my father would tell me war stories that I should have paid more attention to. I considered painting one side of my car really nice because the body was unblemished on that side. The other side had a bunch of dents. Then I'd paint our business name on the car and put "Before" on the bad side and "After" on the good side. The VW's 1200 engine had 36 horsepower, which nowadays is not much, even for a motorcycle. But my car did get pretty good mileage and was reliable. At that time, most Americans drove big cars. Fuel was cheap. My customized VW wasn't for everyone, but it was the perfect vehicle for me.

Starting My Business at Our Shop / Home

Our house in Malibu had a garage at one end and the bedrooms at the

other. It was what they called a "rambler" because it was all one level, built on a cement slab with rooms on either side of a central hallway. The layout bent in the middle where the kitchen and living room met. The bedrooms and living room faced due south, taking in the spectacular 180-degree view of Santa Monica and the Palos Verdes Peninsula on the left, Catalina Island in the center, Santa Barbara Island just to the right of Catalina on a very clear day, and Point Dume to the north, about 12 miles up the coast. The elevation of the house was 500 feet. Catalina Island was 40 miles away. It sat right on the horizon. Growing up with a view like that spoiled me for anywhere else I would ever live.

Our house, built in the 1950s, used a lot of glass. When my dad was working on an art project, he had met Frank Lloyd Wright and Mr. Wright told him to use as many local materials as possible. The house had no insulation at all, and really didn't need any. The roof was such that in the winter the sunlight would cover the entire floor and in the summer the floor was entirely in the shade. The windows fit into groves in the ceiling wood so that the glass was not even noticeable when looking at the roof. This was my parents' dream house where they lived most of their lives.

When I was in high school, my mom said, "Well, we just paid off the house." I asked her how much the monthly payment was, and she said, "$120".

NINE

OCEAN KAYAK BEGINS WITH A LOGO

"Art and design melt into shape and form and the chopper gun"

The identity of my company was hatched from a logo I designed a long time before I truly launched Ocean Kayak. I remember sitting at my dad's desk, gazing at the 1972 Munich Olympics, and designing the logo for Ocean Kayak. Those Olympics were the first to have art figures representing all the different events. That afternoon, the idea of Ocean Kayak being an actual company first hit me. I can still remember the afternoon sun warming the room as I sketched away. The room was a sort of incubator for the creative flow.

Expanding Production to the Carport

Now that I knew a little about fiberglass from building the Girl Scout canoes, I started building many new things at the Malibu carport shop. I made the tandem surfboard kayak there as well as three or four versions of the Scupper.

I also designed and created a special kayak and a new set of fiberglass molds for a guy in Hawaii, Mike Cripps. Mike made his boats in a shop under his parents' house in Kaneohe, on the windward side of Oahu. These kayaks could be popped out of their molds in the morning and the color coat sprayed on right after. As that coat was hardening, the edges of the kayak were trimmed with a skill saw. The top and bottom had already been attached together the day before. After trimming, a hatch cover and other hardware were also installed. This took just enough time for the color coat to kick (harden), so that when the trimming and fitting was finished, the  fiberglass layer could be applied with resin and fiberglass to the top and bottom molds. A short time after the top and bottom were laid up, thickened resin could be applied around the edges and the bottom went down on top of the top mold and the two were clamped together. The new boat was left to harden overnight and then the process would be repeated. This project spread my designs all over Hawaii. And, as an added plus, I come could visit and write it off as a business expense.

My Kayaks Line Up on Dog Beach

Suddenly there were others that wanted to venture out into the ocean and wanted to buy a kayak to do it in. The one-mile long beach I was living on was called Dog Beach. Eventually, I counted 25 kayaks that I sold there. If I sold 25 in one mile of beach, how many miles of beach were there in the world? Fast forward: after years of trial and error (a lot of error), Ocean Kayak was making over 200 of these kayaks a day! My company sold kayaks all over the world. On a recent trip to Dubai in the Middle East I counted 25 sit on top design kayaks on less than a mile of beach!

The UCLA Dive Club and the Garage Sale

C.L. Hager worked at UCLA and ran the Dive Club there. He started using my fiberglass kayaks and would sell them to people in the club. One time he sold one right off the top of his pickup truck to someone who had never seen them before. At the end of the year, we counted that he had sold over 60 of them. If I had too many kayaks and not enough money, I would position myself out on the Malibu highway on a Saturday morning about 8:00 or 9:00 a.m., when locals were doing their errands and not in too much of a hurry. I put up a sign that said "Garage Sale Kayaks." People would pull over before they had a chance to think about what they were doing and a surprising number of people bought my kayaks. I could usually average selling three of them before 1:00 p.m. After that, the out of town beach traffic took over. If I put potential buyers in the kayaks right on the beach and they went through the surf, 50% of them would buy a kayak. The buyers weren't all guys, either. Kayaks were very liberating for women because they could do it themselves.

From Kayaks to Rowboats

I even undertook a rowboat project. This was for Stuart Blue, who saw that my kayaks were selling. He had Jerry Hurst help him simplify a large Whitehall rowboat. It was 17 feet long by 5 feet wide but still quite fast because the waterline was full length but narrower than the top five-foot width of the boat. The rowboat even had a sail.

The idea for the new rowboat he wanted me to build was to create a mold from a wooden prototype that was only three feet wide. It looked more like a canoe but the bow and stern were straight up and down. From the rear, the stern was curved like half an hourglass or a rowboat stern, not pointed like a canoe. The new smaller design had a sliding seat and fittings for outriggers and oarlocks. The oarlocks were placed about eight inches outside the edge of the hull but they could be easily removed for docking.

I made a top deck that looked nice and, of course, spent too much time on it, but eventually made the whole set of molds. Then I proceeded to make five of these boats for Stu. I kept one because it didn't come out very well. Unfortunately, Stu could not sell them and bailed out of the rowboat business, selling it to a company in eastern Washington State.

Washington State seemed like a long way away. These boats were fast and pretty light and could take one rower alone in the middle or one rower sitting forward and facing a passenger in the back. The bottom was completely flat and the boat didn't handle rough seas well, but was very fast. In flat, calm water it flew and also went well in moderate choppy waters.

Fast forward. I later took the extra rowboat to Nuchatlitz, without the sliding seat, and rowed it for a year up there. I eventually brought it back to Bellingham and the kids and I fixed it up and gave it to Rebecca. When I took it down to the local rowboat shop in Bellingham, I saw another almost identical rowboat that my friend Ron Mueller was going to start producing. It turned out that Ron had bought the molds from Graham Boat Works in eastern Washington. The rowboat I helped build had followed me to Bellingham more than 20 years later.

Using a Chopper Gun to Speed up my Fiberglass Kayak Production

I bought a chopper gun, a tool that spit out resin and the harder catalyst, as well as chopping one-inch long glass fibers. When everything was running right, all I had to do was spray the stuff on the molds, roll out the fibers, and let the fiberglass coating harden. For really curvy sections where the foot, butt, and tank well areas were, using the chopper gun was ideal if the coating was applied properly. It was easy to put on too much. The two halves were put together with thickened resin and clamps. I put them together after I took the top and bottom out of the molds. The resin had to be thick like frosting so I used an actual cake decorator to apply a bead of this thickened resin around the outside, then put the top on the hull and clamped them together with many heavy duty little clothespin-type clamps. The thickener I used was asbestos, which was in common use at that time. Once the asbestos was in the resin, there was no dust to contend with. The asbestos made the resin as thick as cake frosting and very strong. After I stopped using asbestos, finding a substitute that worked as well was difficult. It's hard to judge how bad some of these materials really were. I reached another level of professionalism when I could produce two kayaks a day.

Moving the Shop to Yerba Buena

The carport was only about 12 feet wide by 18 feet long and the only way to work when it was cold or rainy was to roll blue tarp curtains down from the roof. I needed to move to a larger, indoor shop. I found an old building with a shop of about 500 square feet at the very north end of Malibu at Yerba Buena Drive, just beyond the Los Angeles county line. This was right across the street from the surf break and very close to Neptune's Net, a place that sold fresh fish and also cooked fresh fish from the large salt-water tanks.

Tim Niemier

TEN

CARE-TAKING A MALIBU BEACH HOUSE

"I find my water tribe who teach me the water dance"

Life was good and became even better when my old boss, Bob Sherman, asked me to take care of his father's house right on the beach in the fancy part of Malibu. Bob's father, Pierce Sherman, was the son of Moses Sherman who pioneered Sherman Oaks in the San Fernando Valley. His father had passed away and the family had the property on the market for sale and didn't want any trespassers moving in or damaging the house. To the south was Doris Day's old house. Just to the left of that house, my neighbor was Stuart Whitman, who acted in a number of westerns and was a real star at the time. A little further down the beach was a house belonging to Andy Williams, the famous singer. I lived a simple life in a fancy beach neighborhood, full of famous people's houses, but the famous people themselves were hardly ever there. When I moved in, I didn't own much. I slept on the front porch and looked east to beautiful sunrises. One time, Bob Sherman came over to say hello and looked in my small refrigerator. Inside were only about three items. Bob was a building contractor who had complicated his life with many possessions. He admired my simplicity.

Living Well on a Shoestring

My VW had a weak battery. My parking spot was about twenty feet long, which enabled me to push the car, jump inside, and pop the clutch to get it started. My weekly routine was to go into Venice to buy eggs that had spots on them for 28 cents a dozen and then go down the street get a loaf of the best day-old sourdough bread for about the same amount. For a few bucks, I was set to make the very best French toast. Dan and I could paddle to a rock where abalones were stacked on top of each other four deep. They were not the gourmet type but the smaller and tougher black abalone, but they were still very good. I noticed a lot of people picking mustard greens near the highway, so I got in the habit of picking them, too. Dan and I read all the Euell Gibbons books on living off the land and seashore. I made great omelets from onions, abalone, mustard greens and my bargain eggs. How could life get any better? I was avoiding someone else's fast game and creating my own.

From Paddling Kayaks to Sailing Outriggers

Life did get even better. Bob Sherman gave me his old rotting Malibu Outrigger. Bob was too busy to fix his old boat and since they were selling his dad's beach house, the sailing outrigger had to go. It needed a whole new hull. I located one for $125 from the bargain box in the Santa Monica paper. For the next few months I worked on that boat at my parents' house. I got a lot of advice from my neighbor and top outrigger sailor, Norm Marchmont, who had moved up to another faster catamaran class called the P-Cat. Warren Miller of ski movie fame also sailed P-Cats.

The Malibu Outrigger was all wood, covered in a thin layer of fiberglass, so there was a lot of fine woodwork to be done. It was a classic sailboat because the mast and arms would bend in the wind with no wires or stays to get in the way. It also had a large 200 sq. ft. sail that was really good in light winds. I was really excited about the price but also excited because this boat actually could haul something in the large main hull, unlike the Hobie Cats, which had just come out but had no storage capacity. Another guy who said he knew how to sail helped me take the Outrigger up the coast. Unfortunately, that day we didn't notice that the wind was blowing pretty hard. The boat flipped when we were a few miles offshore. We flipped it back upright, but didn't release the main sheet or the rope holding in the sail, so after the boat flipped upright, the sail filled and the Outrigger sailed away without us.

We would have been in real trouble if it weren't for the fact that the wind was so strong that it flipped the Outrigger again, not far from where we were treading water. This time, before we righted it, we released the sail, climbed back onboard, and sailed home. Clearly, I needed some instruction. Bob sent me to the Malibu Yacht Club down the beach, where there was a fleet of outriggers and other catamarans. Life was about to get much better.

Finding My Tribe: The Malibu Yacht Club

The Malibu Yacht Club wasn't what you might think of when imagining a proper yacht club with members dressed in white pants and dark blue blazers. It was just a vacant lot with about 50 multi-hull sailboats of various types and sizes and a few buildings with no roofs on them. I could walk there from the beach house. Dues were very cheap. I went to one of their meetings and found all the people to be regular middle class  family types who shared a passion for the ocean. All the people sailing the outriggers were at least ten years older than I. The outriggers were some of the first boats created right in Malibu, mostly by their owners. They weren't sold commercially, but there were a few master builders who built them one at a time or repaired broken parts.

I had ventured into a very special group of people who had a very special meeting place. This was also a very special time when the California lifestyle was defining itself. The MYC was like a weekend tribe. It was not a group you could buy your way into. The club was a great place to hang out in a completely different world separated from surrounding properties only by a hedge of shrubby trees. The members loved the challenges of launching through the surf and they were masters at the art of sailing small sailboats in the big ocean. They were also masters at living life to the fullest. The stories never end. Matt Kivlin was one of the original surfers at Malibu and a regular at the MYC. Surfer Magazine called him the "father of modern style" for surfing.

I was welcomed into the group like I'd just washed up on a South Pacific island; the club really had that flavor of friendliness. The older outrigger guys welcomed the new blood into their ranks. They taught me how to race, which was a great way to learn how to handle this unusual sailboat. Being an outrigger, it sailed differently when the wind was on one side

71

or the other. When the outrigger was to windward, the boat could flip over more easily so the crew had to hike out or move further out to keep the outrigger on the water to power up the sail.

Danny Israel had a nice lightweight red outrigger that usually came in first. Hans Millinaar was usually close behind him with another great boat. Hans was Dutch and loved to explore on the water and had all the systems down pat. He could easily load the boat on a trailer and take it off again, taking only 45 minutes, which all came in handy when we went to places like Mexico. I recently visited Hans. He now sails a trimaran he launches from a trailer and has sailed up and down both coasts of the U.S. over the years.

Another MYC member was Hoyle Schweitzer, who was instrumental in introducing the sailboard to the world with his partner, Jim Drake. Their

company was called Windsurfer International. When I first met Hoyle, he had made a few boards with a sail attached with a flexible joint to a large surfboard that he first called the Baja Board. Gary Seaman shaped the original Baja Board. At that time only a few guys loved the idea of windsurfing. Most people thought it was weird.

Allen Parducci took one of the original fiberglass models to the South Pacific and sailed around Chuuk, then called Truk Lagoon, and told me I really had to go there. Allen was a psychology professor who actually studied happiness at

UCLA. Hoyle's wife Diane was also very active in the business, and after a lot of hard work their windsurfer started to get popular. Hoyle took a trip around the entire U.S. and personally promoted the product. In its heyday, Windsurfer International produced 1200 boards a week. It was beyond my wildest dreams that I could ever make that many.

Later I designed a sailboard that also paddled, which I thought was the only way of becoming a part of a larger class of watercraft. Hoyle told me how easy it was to make them from this plastic that was very different than fiberglass: polyethylene. This information would become extremely important to me later in my career, but switching materials seemed at the time too far a reach for me.

When I first had a real kayak shop in an industrial area to the north of Malibu, I would drive my camper down and spend the whole weekend at the MYC. I could never quite get past all the city regulations about fiberglass production, but I kept building kayaks anyway.

73

During the week, I lived in my small camper outside the shop in the industrial area. Then I met Luise from Canada who had just arrived in Malibu after a long drive with another friend, Nancy, who later helped start Ocean Kayak in the 1980s. Luise and I moved right into the old MYC for a week or so. The MYC had a hot shower and outdoor kitchen with a fridge and a flush toilet so it wasn't that bad. It was also right on the beach.

I did however become very motivated to find a rental house. Eventually I found a converted horse tack room that was small but cute and pretty cheap. There was a large yard out in front that was good for kayak assembly. I found a company to make the two halves of the fiberglass kayaks, and then I would assemble them there.

My landlord was a landscaper who had plants all around the yard there that made it look like a jungle. There were avocado trees, which had lots of fresh avocados for the picking. Driving in involved crossing a creek, which would occasionally get too deep to drive through. One time I took sawhorses out in the shallow creek in the summer time, put a piece of plywood on them and slept in the middle of the creek, enjoying its restful sounds. The

same sawhorses and plywood became a big banquet table for all of the seafood I would bring home from our diving trips. Sometimes I would take all the fresh seafood we had just caught and share at the MYC, if it were a Sunday when everyone was around.

Marriage Happens and Kayak Production Goes On Hold

At the MYC, I had noticed a particularly attractive young girl who was going out with a friend of mine from grade school, Gary Strauss. Gary was a really hot catamaran sailor who sold a boat similar to the Hobie Cat, called the Prindle Cat. This girl would sail with Gary in the races on the weekends. Her name was Rebecca Broward, and she would come over to Malibu from the San Fernando Valley with her parents. I didn't know the family very well at that time but for a while they were absent, and I learned that the whole family had taken their small 36-foot wooden sailboat to Tahiti and Hawaii for two years.

Rebecca Broward returned home, and I was amazed with the family's slide show, portraying the trip as a real adventure. To keep the long slide show from getting too boring, Rebecca's father would interject a slide of a nude Tahitian once in a while. The family did the whole trip on not too much money, working along the way. My friend sent them a $20 bill in the mail to Tahiti. Rebecca and I eventually found each other, fell in love, and shared our love for the ocean.

It was a perfect time for both of us, and it meant a lot to my parents to see me get married and assume a somewhat normal life. Also we shared many of the same friends from the MYC, which was like an extended family by now. Many people were really happy for us. We did tons of outdoor activities and even paddled from Santa Barbara to San Diego, which was about 200 miles down the coast. We would camp on the beach or at the various yacht clubs in the harbors.

I decided to work in the construction trade, building houses and doing remodels for a while at $11 per hour, which was a decent wage in the early 1980s. I worked for a friend Greg Hine. Greg was also the best man at Rebecca and my wedding. I met him at the Malibu Yacht Club who built his own ultra fast and light wood catamaran. A good friend from the MYC was Jerry Hurst, who loved boats and living simply. He was really into TM or Transcendental Meditation, so we learned how to do that from another instructor. I have been meditating ever since. I think it's a good practice that has a lot of healthful benefits. Rebecca and I were ready for an adventure of our own, so we decided to live in the wilds of Canada's west coast on a little island I had bought earlier, called Nuchatlitz. Rebecca's mother Ruth would then refer to Rebecca as "My daughter the immigrant."

Reflections

Enter the Craftsman and the Lover

Struggling to find my place in life, I used my hands-on skills and tried to establish myself as an entrepreneur. Selling the first kayak I created was a major boost to my ego, and seeing how my creations helped get people out and onto the water was a thrill. The major archetype for this chapter of my life is Jung's Magician, or as I will call it here, the Craftsman. For me, The Craftsman is the one who can carve or assemble or put together an object that is not that difficult to build if all the steps are broken down. To a non-Craftsman, this may seem like magic when the final product is finally complete. I feel alive and fully energized when I become the Craftsman. Coming to grips with my childhood and whoever I was, good or bad, enabled me to access my Dreamer, drove my passion, and awoke my mature Lover when I met Rebecca.

MYC was my oasis, in the literal desert of southern California that drove my ADD to distraction and insanity. Moving to a place called Nuchatlitz on Canada's wild west coast was a step that my Hunter could not wait to do. This place was like the MYC with 1000% more wildlife, with only a dozen or so people. The nearest dirt road was 20 miles away by water. Let the adventure begin. Ocean Kayak would have to take a break for a while.

ELEVEN

A MAGICAL PLACE CALLED NUCHATLITZ

"Paradise is really only a state of mind"

Around 1972, I would hang out at the DeVault's dining room table, the social center of their house. The table was placed directly between the living room and kitchen. There was a little pass-through countertop area close to the kitchen sink where plates of food could be handed out for the meal or dishes could be returned directly into the sink after the meal. The living room was a full row of sliding glass windows with a deck and big overhanging roof. Dan's father, George DeVault, was an extraordinary landscape architect and worked hard at keeping the outside plants healthy and beautiful. On the weekend mornings, he was out in the yard rooting around. Later, in the heat of the afternoon after the fog would burn off and he would start to really sweat, he would retire to the smallish TV area on the other side of the kitchen to have a beer and watch some sports on the television.

At this time, I believe Dan was entering his last year at UCLA where he was majoring in Eco studies, which included an amazing amount of biology. Dan had no trouble acing all the classes and getting mostly A's. I struggled with academics but was good with my hands and building things. When we worked together, I would throw the instructions down and start fitting parts together. Dan would pick up the instructions and hand me the next part. We didn't need to discuss the process; we worked well together.

Another life-changing letter arrived at the DeVault's house from Bob DeVault, Dan's cousin in Canada. Bob wanted to know if we might be interested in buying part of an island on the west coast of British Columbia. It was the first letter to change the course of my life. At that time I was building the kayaks out of fiberglass, one at a time. The business paid the bills, but wasn't turning into a career yet. Fortunately, my expenses were pretty minimal.

Bob and Dan DeVault shared the same grandfather who lived in a sort of converted garage in the lower part of the DeVault's house in California. Gramps was an inventor who built the dies to make a blade for a unique potato peeler. He had a small but full machine shop with a lathe, drill press, and many other large power tools. He lived in the single bedroom next to the shop. Sometime he would wander over and have Thanksgiving at our house, probably because he didn't like long car rides.

Dan's cousin Bob had grown up in Sierra Madre near Pasadena. His father, also named Bob DeVault, was George's older brother and an engineer. I believe he had his doctorate in ducted fans for airplanes and props that went in the water used for tugboats. Bob Sr. was brilliant with small model flying devices. The two brothers, George and Bob Sr., invented a toy helicopter that was purchased by a toy company and was sold everywhere at that time, much like the drone of today but without the computer controls.

Bob Jr. was about five years older than I was. Like many young American men of the era, he moved to Canada to make sure that he didn't end up in Viet Nam. The politics around the war were intense. Bob Jr. faced never returning to the US. It wasn't till President Carter declared an amnesty that Bob could return legally. At the time, I even wondered if I should have kids because I thought the world wouldn't make it past the year 2000. Fortunately, Canada was a little more relaxed about issues like Viet Nam.

Visits to Canada

Dan and I had taken several long driving trips to Canada in Grandpa DeVault's old 1965 VW Beetle. Gramps had an old Morris Minor (it looked like a London taxi cab) before that. Our neighborhood had its share of weird cars.

In British Columbia, we car-camped and hiked. This rugged coastal part of southwest Canada was full of rocky inlets like Maine, but not as many beaches as California. Nature was almost overpowering. Eagles were everywhere. At low tide we could get small pinto abalone right off the rocks. We drank Bob's homebrew beer. One night, I remember rowing across the bay at 10:30 p.m. when it was still warm twilight. This place was magical and so different from California with no freeways or freeway lifestyle.

We visited Bob on Vancouver Island in the village of Bamfield, about a third of the way up the island's west coast, right on the open ocean. Bamfield was an old fishing town of a few hundred people, settled in earlier fishing days when small fishing boats would troll for salmon with about six lines in the water. A lot of tall Swedish folks lived there. There was also a separate native community close by, now called a "First Nations" community in Canada. The local machine shop, owned by Mr. Linstrom, had a lathe that could turn propeller shafts over 20 feet in length.

Around town, Bob DeVault was known as "Hippie Bob." When we visited him one summer, he was caretaking a house built from wood that washed up on the beaches. I remember warm summer afternoons that never seemed to end because of the long hours of daylight. That far north, and facing the setting the sun, afternoons would drift into long twilights and it would take forever to get dark. The air was always full of that clean ocean smell.

Hiking the West Coast Trail

On Vancouver Island, Bob had a string of friends who were either Canadian drop outs escaping the big city of Vancouver or other draft dodgers from the US. Originally there was no road to Bamfield. When we were there, a small dirt road provided access. Even today the road is not paved. There was even an old trail from Bamfield that went south and was originally called the Lifesaving Trail. The government built the 77-kilometer trail with warming huts along the route to aid survivors of shipwrecks of the past. Before the trail was built, many early ships would  run aground on the west coast of Vancouver Island from the onshore storm winds from the south. The survivors who made it to shore often died of exposure in the dense woods before they could reach civilization.

Now called the West Coast Trail, the route traverses beaches, climbs up and down steep cliffs, crosses rivers, and meanders through the beautiful rainforest. It rains a lot there which made everything so lush and made the trees huge. When we hiked the trail, a storm came through and kept us in our tent for some time with nothing to read except the First Aid Manual. The next morning, the six-inch-deep cooking pot we'd left outside was full and overflowing. The surf right in front of us was huge and crashing on the rocks. What a place!

Our plan was to hike halfway down the trail and then come back because there was a charge to get across a little narrows there and, if we hiked to the other end, we'd have to get a ride all the way back to where we started. After the huge rainstorm, we came to the river we had crossed just days earlier when it was smaller. Now that same river

was 150 feet wide. We could see that the rope we used to pull ourselves on a raft across was no longer strung up. On closer inspection, we found the rope was lying limply on our side of the river and so was the raft. There was no way we could pull ourselves across the water. With us in our predicament were two brothers we met in a hut that looked out at our river crossing. There was a hot fire burning in the woodstove.

I swam a lot in California, so I volunteered to tie the rope to my waist and swim to the other side. I started as far upstream as I could, jumped into the swift current of cold water, and barely managed to reach the other side and tie the rope there. When I got back, the warming hut was most welcome.

The weather got better. The suspension bridges, which were over 50 feet in the air, were in bad shape, with slippery moss and broken planks, but it was sunny and the place was beautiful and that was all that mattered.

Recently I hiked the whole trail. This time it cost me $120 for a permit. I thought having been made too civilized and easy, unlike years ago when we had quite the adventure, would probably ruin the trail. It turned out there had been a windstorm that winter that dropped over 1000 trees on the trail. They were pretty well cleared and the bridges were heavy-duty steel affairs and much safer. There were still slippery wood-planked trails as well as overused dirt ones. The trail was worn down as far as two feet between the roots of giant trees. This all conspired to make it a huge obstacle course.

TWELVE

FINDING PARADISE

"Paradise becomes reality or visa versa
only after much more work than originally anticipated"

Bob eventually got tired of renting in Bamfield and started looking for his own place to settle on the west coast of Vancouver Island. He got a list of all the privately owned places along the coast. The list was only one page long. British Columbia was originally set up like a colony of Britain to extract resources. To this day, you see photos of the queen in public places and hear British and Scottish words and accents in conversation, like saying "Eh?" at the end of sentences. Much of Vancouver Island is designated as "Crown Land," the equivalent of our national forests, and BLM (Bureau of Land Management) lands in the United States. There were only a few properties that were sold to commercial interests. Our island was part of a company that would buy fish from the commercial fishermen and sell them fuel. This is why the list was so short.

Eventually Bob found a 60-acre island called Nuchatlitz, located about 100 miles northwest of Bamfield, about two-thirds of the way up the coast near the northwest end. Nuchatlitz was a small island near Nootka Island. At low tide, you could walk from one island to the other. Nootka was the native word for "you can go around it." On the south end of Nootka Island was a place called Friendly Cove, where a band of Indians called Moachat lived. They are part of the Nu Chat Nulth band that inhabits the whole area. This area is so rich in food that it is one of the only places in North America that the native people didn't have to be nomadic, chasing their food from season to season

Captain Cook landed in this area and the British claimed the land, although the Spanish were already there and had named the inlets with Spanish names. In Nootka Sound there is a Bligh Island, named for William Bligh, the notorious captain of Mutiny on the Bounty fame.

After Captain Cook, another ship anchored in "Friendly Cove," which was the main native village. The captain said some rather derogatory things about the natives in front of them. Turned out the natives could understand more than the captain anticipated. Chief Maquinna ordered his warriors to kill everyone on the ship and burn it. Two white survivors from the ship were spared. A young blacksmith named James Jewett fascinated Maquinna, so the chief kept him alive for a few years and even gave him a wife. Jewett kept a diary, which was a fascinating account of life on the coast before the Europeans arrived. The book is called "The diary of James Jewett".

Nuchatlitz Island was bigger than Bob could settle alone. Bob got a group together in Bamfield and reached out to others, including Dan's parents. The whole island was 60 acres and sold for $80,000. If we divided it up into roughly 5-acre parcels, the cost would only be $7,200 each. Back at the DeVaults, I thought to myself that maybe even I could afford that. (Remember that at the time, many items were one-tenth the cost that they are now, so that price was like $72,000 in today's dollars.) I was 22, and that was a lot of money. To make the price more challenging, the group decided to pay off the sales price in only two years, or two payments of $3,600 each.

This letter arrived just before Dan went back to UCLA and we wanted to see the island before someone else got it. We hopped in my VW beetle, converted to a truck with a very small camper, and headed north with our mighty 36 horsepower motor powering us and two sit-on-top kayaks up the I-5 freeway. We met up with Bob in a town inland from Bamfield, called Port Alberni.

Paddling to Nuchatlitz for the First Time

Bob was living with a French Canadian girl named Monique, who was unafraid of anything. She was perfect for the role of pioneer woman. The very next morning we took off and drove for hours up the east side of Vancouver Island because the west side had so many inlets and high mountains that roads were not an option.

It was an unusually warm dry afternoon when we arrived at Tahsis, a small town of about 2000 people. The town can receive well over 10 feet of rain a year. The 40 mile dirt road was very rough and all the trees had been recently logged off, so it looked like the area had been bombed. The town had a mill and logs stacked all over. We parked the VW and put our sit-on-top California-style kayaks in the water and headed down the inlet.

Rock cliffs rose up on both sides of the fjord on either side of us. As the sun set in front of us, we could see the twisted trees of the open coast 10 miles ahead. We had already paddled 10 miles. As we approached the end of the inlet, everything changed. The scenery looked like a huge Japanese Garden with Bonsai trees on every little island and mossy rock.

We pulled in to camp at a small beach filled with beach logs. The night sky cooled off the warm rocks as our campfire flickered. We were tired.

The next morning, we got up with the sun glaring. We got out our map and located Nuchatlitz, only about a mile away through an incredible maze of islands and intertidal landscapes. The immense forest and the open ocean were incredible. Great blue herons flew over like giant prehistoric creatures. Bald eagles were everywhere. We slept out on the rocks and bonded with the dream of living out there. There was no turning back now. This place had gotten under our skin. The idea of living in the wilderness seemed too good to be true. Somehow we did it.

Dan's parents fronted him the money on the promise that he would finish school. I was on my own. Friends in California soon referred to me as the guy who "owned his own island."

Living the Nomad Life Between California and Canada

For the next few years, I developed a lifestyle where I would try to go north as early as I could manage in the spring to spend summers up in Nuchatlitz and slowly work my way south in the fall to winter in California. I saw different friends on different trips, and, as time passed, on each trip I saw a new chapter of various people's lives. Their kids would be a foot or two taller, or sometimes the family would even have split up. One time I rowed at about eight locations on the way down the coast, using the same rowboat that got us out to the island and back. This yearly pilgrimage kept me in touch with my larger family of friends.

Making a Home from the Land

When I was much younger, one movie that had a huge impact on me was Swiss Family Robinson. The idea of living off the land in a wilderness environment greatly appealed to me. I wanted to do just that. Our island life on the remote Canadian coast was the perfect place to make that dream come true. The time I spent in this area was so full of "now" moments that it felt like when I went to Disneyland as a boy and couldn't believe I was really there. The magic of Nuchatlitz never wore off. It still hasn't to this day.

I explored the endless coastlines and beaches and looked for things that had washed up on shore. I found an oil drum floating about half full with paint thinner-like stuff and another one with heavy gear lube. I used the oil for chainsaw bar oil and thinned it with the paint thinner to make oil for spraying on rusty tools to make them work better. The beaches were full of logs that I would gather for firewood. Some of the cedar logs I would saw in two and put boards on them crossways to make ramps and walkways. There was also Asian trash of all sorts on our beaches

from all over the Pacific Rim. I later learned this was from the North Pacific Gyre (aka the Great Pacific Garbage Patch), an island of plastic and garbage that gets stuck in the middle of the Pacific Ocean and occasionally spills out on beaches like ours.

When marriage, my kids, and Ocean Kayak came along, my trips to Nuchatlitz became more infrequent because I was so busy with the outside world. Some years I would have a building project all organized like I was launching an attack. I would work feverishly and leave exhausted but I felt good about my accomplishments. Later I would just go to the island and not do anything more than hike or boat around.

The Nuchatlitz Twelve

Twelve of us bought into this island as a group in 1973. We formed a corporation called Nuchatlitz Enterprises. We owned shares in the corporation that entitled us to our designated piece of land on the island. We all had different ideas about what this place was for us. Some people lived there, building docks and making improvements. Others came out for only a week each year and wanted to keep everything untouched. Some didn't visit for years, but the very thought of owning this wonderful place gave them peace of mind in their day-to-day living wherever that might be.

These different groups and desires sometimes caused a little friction that lingered like any family drama. Every year we had an annual meeting when the island's population would go from two or three people to fifteen. These meetings still feel like an awkward Christmas dinner with the distant relatives you haven't seen for a year. The atmosphere is tense until the party after the meeting, when the wine starts flowing. Most of the people were from the original group of twelve. The people who normally lived in other places, and only came out for the meeting, would be amazed at the sudden population explosion on our island and wanted to limit any more growth. The people who always lived on Nuchatlitz welcomed the activity. A few days after the meeting, the people who lived elsewhere would go home and the island would return to a population of three and peace would reign again.

I think it is amazing that we are still talking to each other after 40 years. I wonder what will happen when we aren't around to maintain our utopia anymore. Younger people nowadays prefer to be in more populated areas and aren't as interested in the back-to-nature lifestyle we experimented with. There is only one of the kids of all of the members (who are all over 60 years old now) who have spent more than two weeks on the island alone. Anyone interested?

THIRTEEN

BUILDING MY HOUSE ON THE ISLAND

"Nothing would ever get built or babies born
if we knew how much work it really takes"

I finally decided it was my turn to build a house in Nuchatlitz. Lumber from the local mill was $60 for 1000 board feet, so for a few hundred bucks for siding and nails I could get a truckload of hemlock for framing as well as some really nice cedar. Luckily wood floats, and I paid Paul Smith, a native fisherman, to tow it down the inlet with his 36-foot fishing boat. The propeller on his boat was three feet in diameter. All the rest of the windows, sinks, and everything else, were bought used for a few hundred dollars and the new things like nails, tarpaper, and insulation were pretty minimal. The rest was just a lot of hard work.

Furniture was boated in or salvaged from the Tahsis dump, which seemed to have a steady supply because people were always moving in and out of town. My boat at that time was a huge 22-foot open dory rowboat from the Malibu Yacht Club, built by one of my mentors, Warren Seaman, Gary Seaman's father, who built offshore catamarans in the 1960s to race from California to Hawaii. I got the dory for free because someone had left it in the surf and blew the bottom out. I raised the bottom about six inches, which made the bottom four feet wide instead of just three.

The original rowing dories were made for fishing out on the Grand Banks fishing grounds. They had to stack and were carried out on large old sailing schooners. These rowboats were pretty tippy until they had a few hundred pounds of cod in them. I put a 7.5 horsepower Honda outboard motor on my dory. The boat moved about 10 miles per hour.

At 10 miles per hour, it took me two hours to motor the 20 miles into town and then two hours back. On the way back I would lock the motor and climb into the front and read my mail, steering by leaning one way or the other. I named the boat Caveat Emptor, Latin for "buyer beware." It was a wonderful boat for my needs, but I did not get to have the last laugh because I loaned it to the natives and didn't get paid when they wrecked it.

Wintering at Nuchatlitz

One winter we stayed in Nuchatlitz, which was a real challenge for Rebecca because Christmas time was family time for her. My family was

much less formal and more independent about such things. We selected a Christmas tree and decorated it with shells and washed-up fishing lures. For electricity, we had one car battery and some solar cells. They powered one 12-volt light that was very efficient and too bright to look at so we put it in a round Japanese paper covering, which shielded the brightness but let a beam of pure light out through the hole in the bottom for reading.

The electricity also powered a radio that received backwoods AM channels from all over the U.S., although they would fade in and out. We would listen to old radio shows like Fibber McGee and Molly. We had a little wood stove for heat and cooking, we ate lots of fish, and life was good.

Some days the weather was so stormy and rainy we would just quit and play Scrabble. I invited neighbors Tony and Doreen from the neighboring native reserve over to play Scrabble. Rebecca and I thought we might have to help them with difficult words, but it turned out that they had been dealing with the rain for way longer than we hippies had and they had practiced a lot. It was interesting that our technique was to create obscure word combinations and Doreen's was to effectively use more common words. She won hands down.

The Annual Herring Gold Rush

Every March, the little herring fish would swarm into our little bays in huge numbers and do a mass egg laying and spawning, all over just a few days. The whole bay would turn different colors, first with eggs and then white with herring sperm. Any animal that could eat herring would show up there. I counted over 50 eagles wading in a little stream in front of the house across the tide flat. All the predators would gorge themselves but were still not able to make a dent in all the schools of herring. One week the bay would be empty as it was for most of the winter, and then the next week it would be crowded with more than 100 fishing boats that were 30- to 40-feet long, towing flat 8-foot by 20-foot herring punts. They'd scoop up the herring in nets below and then flip the fish into the punts using attached rollers and beater bars.

Each year the season was open only for a very short period of time so the fishing activity was always frenzied. Before the season was declared open on the VHF Radio by the Fisheries Department, the bay was filled with a whole flotilla of boats and men with nothing to do but drink and carry on. I don't know what they thought of us. I couldn't participate because I couldn't work legally in Canada. Besides, all the crews were picked before the boats ever left home.

Sadly, as fish stocks dwindle, the price usually goes up and fishermen race to catch the last one. One year, the season was open for only about 24 hours, and the average haul made on these little fish was worth $36,000. Most of the fishermen had guns. It was madness. One of the herring punts tried to take a shortcut through the rocks as the tide was rapidly falling. The boat got stuck, an incident which probably cost the

owners $20,000. Other herring punts would get too full and simply sink.

A five-gallon bucket of herring might cost $100. When they were cheaper, we smoked the fish. They tasted like little sausages and were great on pizza instead of pepperoni. A week later all the boats, herring, and eagles were gone and everything was back to normal except there were small-fertilized herring eggs all over the seaweed. They were small and translucent and somehow stuck to the slimy seaweed. The natives really liked these eggs and I found them very rich and pleasing to eat without tasting fishy at all.

Interesting Neighbors at the Reserve

On the Reserve next door, there were two main families: the Smiths and the Michaels. The oldest member on the Reserve was Girl Nan. She wove baskets the traditional way, and spoke only the native tongue. If I was in the  Reserve at mealtime, she would say "chick wa a uuk" which meant

 come and eat. No one knew exactly how old she was. We did know, however, that when she was a little girl there were still longhouses. She must have been alive when the tribes had one of the last battles between two bands up the coast. When we first got to Nuchatlitz, her husband Felix was still alive. He was very funny and spoke English. He told me once about when the dance called the Twist arrived in Nuchatlitz; everyone did it. In his day there were more people in the Reserve and they had a fruit orchard next to the graveyard across the bay.

Another elder at that time was Moses, a 76-year old whose daughter Rose was the wife of Albin, who was the chief of the reserve next to us. I told Moses that I wanted to  immigrate to Canada and asked if he had any idea on how I could do that. It turns out that he knew all the politicians from the last 50 or so years and was very influential. Next thing I knew, the local member of Parliament (the equivalent of a congressman in the U.S.) made a phone appointment with me (we used the phone at the Tahsis Building Centre hardware store in Tahsis, twenty miles away from the island). After we talked, he wrote me a letter of recommendation that really helped when Rebecca and I applied for permanent resident status. This would give us medical coverage and enable us to work. After a lot of bureaucratic paperwork, we got in. It was our dream to live happily ever after in this paradise. I wasn't thinking of making kayaks at this point in my life.

I did various jobs in the area but would still make the trip to California most every year just because it was warmer there and I could work there. I saw nothing wrong with the subsistence living we were doing. Instead of going to work to make money to pay a fisherman to get a fish, I just went out and caught a fish and skipped the middleman. It was really cheap to live there because all you needed was a bunch of rice and simple vegetables like onions and potatoes to round out a meal. For a while, we had a pantry on the north side of the house, which was almost as cold as a refrigerator except in summer. Later, I electrified the house and put in some solar cells and batteries. This meant we could have the conveniences of the outside world very cheaply, even all the way out there. We had all the water we wanted if there was any rain at all, even with our small water tanks. I finally put in two large tanks and a pump that ran off batteries, which meant I would never run out of water. Sometimes it felt like living on Nuchatlitz was like being on a boat, because we were surrounded by water and the weather and seasons were always changing around us. Living right on the water taught me a lot about how to make boats water friendly.

The community out there was connected in different ways. There were no telephones; however, we did all have VHF radios in our houses. These radios were intended for boats, but no one really cared. When someone from the community talked on the main channel 8, everyone else could hear them so we sort of all knew what was going on. During this time, there would be a few other couples around and we'd share about half of our dinners. Sometimes I would even dress up a little. If someone scored a nice salmon, we could all enjoy it fresh. If there was no fish, we would take the fish that we put in jars and make a salmon loaf with a nice pastry crust that also tasted great.

Hauling liquids like beer was expensive and costly, so we brewed our own. I had watched my dad brew beer so I was sort of familiar with the technique. The trick was to make 10 gallons instead of just five gallons, so there would be enough to age for a month or two. If I didn't fuss around, it took me only a few hours to make that much. The hardest part seemed to be cleaning the bottles for bottling day. I eventually chose 16-ounce pop bottles with the screw lids, which I would reuse.

After drinking, I would just rinse the bottles out and put a little tissue in the top to keep out the dust. For a few bucks a gallon, I was happy.

Getting Back into the Kayak Business

Rebecca and I were thinking of getting back into the kayak business. We thought of creating the business in various places in Canada but eventually settled on being in the U.S. just across the border in Bellingham. We ran into a couple Rebecca and her family had met in the South Pacific on their sailing trip. This meeting resulted in Rebecca's parents moving up to the Bellingham area and building a house, so we had connections there. Rebecca's parents Ruth and Paul had grown weary of being in L.A. because it had grown pretty stressful there, as the city had changed over the years.

To develop the kayak business this time, we wanted to make them out of rotomolded polyethylene like Hoyle Schweitzer did with his windsurfers. At this time, Hoyle was doing very well and making 1200 boards a week. I knew that we could never produce anywhere near this number using fiberglass. I didn't know the first thing about this new plastic but was willing to learn. The other tipping point was that we were now pregnant. I think when that happened, my nesting provider instinct kicked in and I became driven like I had never been before to succeed in business.

Reflections

How Living in Nature Affects My Life

I still own my place at Nuchatlitz. I return there whenever I need to recharge my spiritual batteries. No matter what else was going on in my life, the days I spent at Nuchatlitz were always precious. I am so glad that I did not wait until retirement to achieve my big dream of living in tune with nature.

When you are unplugged, off the grid, and living with nature, you have no choice but to be firmly present in the here and now. Whether or not your business is flourishing doesn't seem important. Whether or not you have ADD or other issues doesn't matter.

I believe that following my passions at Nuchatlitz helped me in all the other areas of my life, too. Do you have a safe natural place like that where you can escape and have the freedom simply to think and to be? It's better than any tranquilizer, alcohol, or drugs. When you have a place you have been that makes you think of peaceful thoughts, just knowing it is there can help one get through the stresses of life.

FOURTEEN

BUILDING OCEAN KAYAK, AGAIN

*"If you're gone do it, gone do it right
even if it ain't quite right the first time round."*

We were committed to making another go at creating Ocean Kayak. The
vision seemed completely clear. We could feel it. We were married now
and I had much more confidence and focus because I was not alone. I
also had the moral support of a great beach tribe at the Malibu Yacht
Club, as well as other friends who believed my dream would become
reality. They were my mentors and true watermen and women. They
led me to my ultimate love, the water. They showed me how to love
this mysterious part of nature and of myself. My fears and passions

were all swimming around in the depths. My soul had already been taken hostage, and I was completely in love, with no turning back from my mission. What would I find when I dove deep? I held my breath.

My career might never have gotten off the ground without all the mentors I found in the Malibu Yacht Club. One of the members, Hoyle Schweitzer (who introduced the windsurfer to the world) had an influence on my kayak building process. Until he built his own factory, Hoyle's windsurfers were rotomolded (rotational molded) by another mentor of mine, Elmer Good, who was a pioneer in the rotomolding industry. The windsurfer was the first mass-market product that was rotomolded and was a huge success.

My mentors had let the genie out of the bottle by making a large surfboard and sail that was both durable and affordable. Our world would never be the same because now almost everyone could dance on the water.

Using windsurfers, people all over the world became intimate with the water and the wind. Even my friend Dan DeVault got a windsurfer and claimed he could be a member of the Pepsi Generation way up at Nuchatlitz. People in France were now surfers. A guy with a windsurfer and an old Fiat had more appeal to women than a guy with a new Mercedes. When I ask Europeans if they want to be like an American, they say, "No." But if I ask them if they would like to surf in California, they say, "Sure!"

Bob Jensen, a guy who worked for Hoyle, told me I could make a mold for rotomolding a kayak. By chance, Bob had shown up at a garage sale I was having and simply said, "You could make your own mold." I believed him and I did just that. One person can turn an idea into reality by believing in it and having the vision and faith that it will work.

Bob had been a pretty well known surfboard shaper before he shaped boards for Hoyle's Windsurfer. Hoyle's boards were made with aluminum molds that were hammered out of flat sheets of aluminum. Bob would hand shape a board from hardwood for the mold makers. The mold makers were auto body guys from New Zealand called "panel beaters". They would work the aluminum around Bob's board, shaping the metal into the finished molds.

Deciding to Go For It

When do you decide to risk everything and go for broke? I can't remember the exact moment it happened, but one day Rebecca and I decided to go for it. For me, that meant getting back into the kayak business. For Rebecca, it meant diving into a business  that was completely new to her. She probably didn't have any fear because she hadn't been in that business before. I guess I feel like I can do all kinds of things with a team. I need to have someone else say,

"Let's go for it." It's odd that one minute I don't think something is possible and the next minute I believe it can happen, and it does, just because someone tells me it can.

Prototype Number 1: A Kayak that Sails or a Windsurfer than Can Be Paddled

My original idea was to make a Windsurfer that paddled because I considered the Windsurfing market to be many times bigger than the kayak market. At that time there were virtually no shops in Southern California that sold kayaks or even canoes for that matter. Most people made their own boats out of  fiberglass through clubs or on their own. The magazine Popular Mechanics had plans and articles for such things. Nowadays, most anything is for sale if one just looks hard enough on the Internet.

Our first kayak prototype was intended to look like a Windsurfer. I made a full-sized prototype board that was over six inches thick and had a slight "V" to the hull like the international class of sailboard that was called the Pan Am class. These boards were designed to sail in all wind speeds, so they were pretty long. The board I hand shaped from Styrofoam and coated like a surfboard with an epoxy fiberglass skin went really well under paddle power and was fast using the sailboard sail. But it seemed a bit long, so I took about a foot off the tail and it moved even better.

Bob Jensen really liked the shape, which meant a lot to me. The board even surfed reasonably well. This hybrid sailing kayak was our first prototype for this new venture.

The Windsurfing Industry Gets Too Specialized

Sailboarding/windsurfing had grown very fast as a sport, and taken a few different directions. Windsurfers were getting faster and faster. The boards were getting smaller. Experts would dance on huge waves in Hawaii, and could even power ahead of the waves. These boards were breaking the speed records for any type of craft on the water. Gary Seaman shaped out the first windsurfer called the Baja Board. He also made a small, very speedy sailboard that held the world record for a short time at somewhere around 40 MPH. Soon no one wanted the original windsurfer because there were so many new shapes. To get the best performance, windsurfers needed more wind, which meant that people drove a long way to find the perfect high wind conditions. Because the new boards were smaller, they sank when the rider stood on them and tried to lift the sail out of the water, so surfers had to lie down in the water and let the wind lift body and sail up. This is where windsurfers lost interest for me. I thought twice about making a kayak that would fit into a sport that was becoming an "expert only" sport. A kayak that was truly "water-friendly".

FIFTEEN

A SIT-ON-TOP KAYAK

"The idea of a plastic sit on top kayak is so simply beautiful but the harsh physical reality of things that don't work is the slap in the face that lets you know you are alive here and now."

Now the plan was to make a sit-on-top kayak more like my fiberglass Scupper. The shape would be stronger if it were hollow inside. The prototype sailboards were hand shaped from foam, which made the whole craft more difficult and expensive to build. The only major change we made was to add a hatch in the rear instead of creating a tank well like I had built to carry my scuba gear.

Before tackling rotomolding, we decided to make the kayaks first out of fiberglass to pay for the rotomolds. We hired a few young guys to work for us, but fiber glassing proved to require much more experience than these guys had. Then one of them who claimed to be devoutly religious simply disappeared one day after borrowing money from all of his friends. So far, my "team" was not exactly pulling together so we quickly moved to Plan B.

We abandoned our attempts to make and sell the fiberglass model, and instead put all of our efforts into making these kayaks out of rotomolded polyethylene. Now I was fully committed to making this leap into a totally new more durable but more flexible material and way of manufacturing that I had never done before. I hoped my experience with designing fiberglass kayaks would translate well into this new medium. We were going for broke and committed to going into serious rotomolded production.

Naming the New Kayaks

We figured this new type of kayak needed a name. The phrase "sit-on-top" had not been invented yet. Rebecca came up with the name Scupper because a scupper is an opening in a sailboat that drains the deck or cockpit area if water fills it. Rebecca was very familiar with this, after cruising the South Pacific on a small sailboat with her family. The foot well or cockpit in a sailboat is not unlike the depressions in a sit-on-top kayak in that the area is above the waterline so water can drain out. These new kayaks were built to plow through the waves but drain, too.

Rotomolding

Rotomolding is a process where polyethylene powder is poured into a metal mold, which is then clamped together and rotated so that the puddle of plastic eventually coats all parts of the inside of the mold. When the mold is heated, the plastic begins to melt and stick to the inside surface of the hot mold, building up in the same way sugar sticks to your wet finger when you put it into the sugar bowl. The plastic powder actually looks like sugar at first on the inside of the mold. Then, as the mold continues to heat up, the powdered plastic melts into a gooey mass about the consistency of peanut butter, hopefully in a perfectly even layer on the inside of the mold. Sometimes, if the mold is too hot, the plastic drips a bit.

After the plastic is all melted, the mold is cooled. The plastic inside solidifies and then starts to shrink about **3.5%**. The shrinkage might not seem like much but turns out to be about 5 inches in a 14-foot kayak. Removing the kayak from the mold at the right stage in the cooling cycle is critical, as well as is putting the kayak in the right cooling fixture. We even added compressed air from a shop vac to the inflate the kayak slightly as it cooled, which gave the kayak more floatation in the water and kept the plastic from sagging before it was completely cool and set.

Learning from the Easily Company

I worked briefly for a small company named Easily, the name of which incorporated the initials of the two owners, Ed Shield and Lyman Young.

I worked for them with the intent of making my own mold. They would make the "patterns" that would be cast into aluminum. If whatever they were trying to create was large, sometimes the resulting pieces had to be welded together, because casting large parts is much more difficult than casting small ones. My first job with Easily was to make patterns for a jet ski accessory mold for a product called The Wedge. The first jet skis were made by Kawasaki. Riding one was like riding a motorcycle and required some skill because they were tippy until they got up some speed. However, most Americans really wanted a jet ski that they could ride the first time in front of their family or friends after a few beers. In other words, the required skill level had to be lowered. The part that would come out of the mold I was working on was a flotation ring around the jet ski that would enable any drunken guy to not look like an idiot in front of friends and family when trying it for the first time. The Wedge even had a seat, so standing was not required.

Making My Ocean Kayak Scupper Mold

I went about making the patterns for my mold completely differently than Easily had done. I had designed and built hundreds of kayaks by then and was pretty familiar with fiber glassing and carving different foams. In the end, my patterns for the jet ski Wedge product worked very well and took only half the time to build, which surprised Ed and Lyman. It even surprised me, because I had never done this before by myself. Everyone was happy and I went on to make my own patterns for the pieces of aluminum that were welded together to make the first Scupper kayak mold.

Along the edge of the mold there were steel pins that were inserted to line up the sides of the molds. The surface of a cast aluminum mold is pretty soft. After grinding, the surface is sandblasted with ball bearings to make it condensed and harder and more durable. This process can warp the mold, so putting it back together can be difficult. Then it gets ground out again which can take days. After that it is heat-treated to make the total mold relax. After a few heat cycles it fits better and better. I reasoned that this type of mold should last a long time if treated properly. Workers and machines had damaged some of the molds that Ed and Lyman made, so I learned what not to do with my mold.

My deal with Ed and Lyman was that they would put the mold together and they got a royalty for helping me with it. I figured that if my mold ever did get damaged, they would want to fix it to keep getting their royalty, sort of like insurance.

Finding a Company to Run the Scupper Mold

It was never my intention to mold my own kayaks. Rotomolding a 14-foot kayak requires a really big oven for the mold to rotate inside of. After the mold was finished, I went to the molding company, who said they could turn the mold in their rotomolding machine. I had to build a huge mold holder to rotate my mold around to all angles. The mold was 15 feet long and weighed 400 pounds. The oven that heated the mold up to 400 degrees was huge. We discovered that they had made a miscalculation and the mold wouldn't fit.

Panic set in and I didn't want to think about it for a few days. This could mean I would have to get a company in central California to make these kayaks, which would be a huge hassle. This also meant that I was forced to do my own rotomolding. I had to make an oven of my own, and quickly, because I was running out of money.

Designing a Rotomolding Machine with No Instructions

After the panic wore off, I started to think, "Well, how hard could making a rotomolding machine really be?"

I came up with a design where the oven would fit around the mold all in one unit. The framework was made from 2x2 inch square tubing I could weld with a cheap arc welder. I heated everything with a propane flame bar underneath. This was sort of like a huge barbeque spit: primitive but effective. I went to the gas place and asked them how burners worked and then faked it. I had no time for engineers who were so exacting about specifications that the machine would never get built. Usually anyone who was supposed to know anything would tell me I was nuts or what I was trying to do was impossible Elmer Good, my rotomolding windsurfer guru, would offer all kinds of support about how to build this or that, and then after something was built, he would ask, "Did it work?" There was only enough time to move forward and make adjustments later. I made the main bearing just steel on steel. It never wore out. I began to work longer and longer days. The machine was coming together. I had no preconceived notions or even knowledge about how to make these things

116

SIXTEEN

WHO NEEDS INSTRUCTIONS?

"There are no instructions the first time it is assembled."

The oven I built had the mold inside of it, permanently. (Typical rotomolding machines used removable molds.) The whole top of my oven had two doors, hinged at the corners, that opened up to allow fans to cool the mold after it was done cooking. I fashioned part of the oven structure to take a hoist attachment to lift off the top part of the cast aluminum mold, which weighed about 200 pounds. The top had to be lifted evenly, or the pins would catch, which could warp the mold.

The burner was connected to a four-foot-tall 100-pound, 30-gallon, propane tank, which heated the mold. Heating the mold was extremely efficient. To heat the 500-pound package, including 40 pounds of plastic, took about 20 minutes and cost about two dollars per kayak. I could heat about 25 kayaks per 100-pound propane cylinder.

In conventional rotomolding, one oven holds a variety of different molds for outside companies. If these companies sell tons of their products, then they purchase ovens and make the products in-house, because then they could save the 30% cost of the rotomolding. I skipped the step of hiring out the rotomolding and made the ovens and mold myself.

The bottom hull mold was bolted in at either end, saving tons of money usually spent on a support system and also made for faster production cycles because there was less inside the oven to heat.

To activate the rotation, I used a variable-speed DC motor to turn at only about 60 rpm, or one turn per second or less. The tilt was activated with a garage door opener with a remote hand-held unit, the type that you'd usually keep in your car. They cost $139.00 and lasted through hundreds of kayaks. With practice, I could replace the modified garage door opener or, "GDO Unit," in about 15 minutes. The "puddle" of polyethylene powder eventually contracts and sticks to create a seamless skin.

Learning How to Make Rotomolding Work for Ocean Kayak

After all the pieces of my rotomolding machine were assembled, we put powder into the mold, fired up the burner and activated the rotations. The plastic all melted; then we cooled it. Finally, we pulled out a deformed looking kayak. Argh!

Terrified, I took the monstrosity to Ed and Lyman. They said it was normal. It turns out that you have to pump air inside the kayak while it cools. We eventually discovered that we could pull the kayaks out of the mold while they were hot and as flexible as leather; that had the advantage of not needing to heat up the mold so much for the next

kayak. While still warm, the molded kayak was like a noodle, so I made a bench that would hold the kayak in the right shape with the right rocker or curvature to the bottom and then, with air pressure applied with a shop vac, the kayak would settle into the perfect shape.

Finally, we could quickly make good kayaks.

Finding Shop Space in Simi Valley

I found industrial space for rent in Simi Valley near the Easily Company, about 50 miles from Malibu. I moved in with some real innovators. The people I rented the space from were rather famous because they had flown a human-powered airplane across the English Channel after winning another human-powered flight prize.

The name of the company was Aerovironment; started by Paul McCready. The company made other things when I was there, including little blimp-style drones with cameras, which attracted a lot of military types to their dog-and-pony demo days. The other really interesting project they had going, just on the other side of the wall from where our machine was cranking out kayaks, was a solar powered car called the "solar racer," which was to race across Australia for General Motors. This was a big secret innovation that we finally got to see when they were done. I loved this creative environment.

Crowd funding, 1986 Style

A friend of mine, Nancy Bennetts, heard that I was making kayaks. She got 25 of her friends together to get a special group deal. I sold the first 25 of my kayaks for $250 each, or $5,000. This advance funding bought enough polyethylene for my first 50 kayaks, which meant I didn't need to take out a bank loan to start up the production line.

For the first few years, I borrowed no money from banks. I got so I could make 10 kayaks in 12 hours all by myself, which was a lot of work but felt sort of like printing $100 dollar bills every hour. Suddenly, we needed our first night shift crew. I was lucky enough to hire Fred DeVault, who was Dan DeVault's younger brother, to run the machine. Fred was a great guy who had hiked with Dan and me many times. He was all heart and did a great job with all my homemade equipment. Leaving the whole shop in the care of anyone, even as much as I trusted Fred, was hard to do. It went well enough to finish our first crowd funded kayaks and get us into business. That's where the fun really began.

Our Home Was Our Office

Rebecca and I lived in a small one-room apartment above a two-car garage located at the other end of Malibu. This place was next door to Roger and Melone Trivet, who had two small boys who I am sure are now taller than I am. Roger was a house builder and remodeler and later helped me get started building our house in Nuchatlitz.

Our apartment became the headquarters of Ocean Kayak as well as our living space. At 8:00 am, our kitchen became the office and we hired our first employee, Sheila, to run the office. Sheila, who had actually gone to finishing school in her youth, was amazing at doing anything and everything. At about 5:00 pm, the office went back to being living space.

I sometimes brought home the cut-off ends of kayaks that had flaws that made then unsalable. I would use the ends for shows or beach demos. Some of the local kids took them up on the grassy hillsides and slid down with the pointy end downhill and the hatch or the cut off end uphill and a little head sticking out. That looked like something I would have tried as a kid, probably dangerous, but a lot of fun.

Working and Driving Too Hard in L.A.

Working in Los Angeles always involves a lot of driving. Commuting between the shop in Simi Valley and my parents' house and our house was more than 100 miles round trip. Even though I had people I could leave the rotomolding machine with, it was still a lot of stress. Through this time period, we did manage to make around 459 kayaks that I stored at my parents' house. Olivia Newton John's significant other was a sportsman. He saw this array of kayaks and bought a few for their beach house.

SEVENTEEN

MOVING TO BELLINGHAM

"But I still miss the sound of chainsaws and the ocean in Canada."

In another pleasant surprise, we found out Rebecca was pregnant with our first child. We had already immigrated to Canada and had medical insurance up there so we decided to have the baby in Canada. I remember it was in the winter and we went up a month or so before the baby was due. We stayed in Victoria at a little place on the water. I had a Scupper there with a little spray skirt that was put on with Velcro tape and kept me warm while I paddled.

I met Harold and Mia Aune, who lived on a trimaran and built rowboats. I showed them the rotomolded kayak I had made. They were envious, because they had been involved with sailboards earlier and knew of

Hoyle Schweitzer's Windsurfer. We also met another young couple that lived by the water's edge with another rowboat. We were excited to have our baby in Canada, but the baby was two weeks overdue.

Nathan

We went in to the doctor's office for routine checks. They said we had to go to the hospital immediately. We learned the baby had no heartbeat. Our son Nathan had died before he was born.

This wasn't in the script. It didn't even seem possible. Now we had to give birth to a baby who was not alive. When Nathan came, he was beautiful. I believe that was the hardest loss I will ever face.

I learned that couples that go through this sort of trauma usually break up from the stress. Rebecca's mother, Ruth, came up to comfort us. Rebecca and Ruth were very close. Eventually we recovered enough to handle it most of the time, but when we explained to others, we would break down regularly. We learned the couple that had the rowboat and lived near us had gone through the same thing and had a lot of emotions still pent up about it. This sort of event is not the sort of thing that is easy to bring up or brag about and that is the sort of culture we live in. As a society, our unhealthy tendency is to bury the thoughts and feelings surrounding tragic events like having your baby die.

We eventually made it back to L.A. We celebrated Mother's and Father's Days without Nathan. We considered ourselves parents nonetheless. It was and still is a painful experience, but it makes me thankful for what I have.

Daring to Try Again

Rebecca and I had some other friends from the coast, Dean and Cindy Smith, who had a very premature baby, Jasper. Jasper had some touch-and-go times but pulled through and eventually was healthy. Why did this unlikely baby make it and ours didn't for no apparent reason? We never got any information about why Nathan had died. We didn't know if we should start trying again to have another child. We were in limbo.

Deciding to Move North

I got busy and got back to making the kayaks. I knew our time and patience were limited in L.A. and I wanted to make the most of it. We knew we were going to move the plant up to Bellingham. I wanted a backlog of kayaks before we left. Everything was going well and the boats kept cranking out of our Simi Valley 2,000-square-foot mini factory. For once something was actually working.

Then the fire marshal did a routine fire check, and I learned that my method for making kayaks was not within fire code. In other words, my kayak-making days in L.A. were over.

Rebecca and I had landed a caretaking gig on another part of the Malibu beach in front of Las Tunas Road. The house was not as fancy as the Sherman house I'd lived in years ago, but it was close to Topanga Beach where I had spent much of my early childhood. The house sat on pilings and when the big waves would storm in, the whole house would rumble.

Around this time we still hadn't heard if it was okay to get pregnant again; we had no idea if another pregnancy would have problems. We decided to try again and succeeded in short order. We still needed to have our baby in Canada because we didn't have health care insurance and couldn't apply for it, because a baby on the way was considered a "preexisting" condition. We worked hard to get the last of the kayaks made in California; then we planned to put the whole factory on a big trailer and head north in time to spend Christmas with Rebecca's parents, who now lived in Bellingham, Washington, just about twenty-five miles south of the Canadian border. Just before we hatched that plan, when Rebecca was only a couple months pregnant, we had a scary incident with an intruder at the beach house, which may have hastened our decision to move out.

We left California the day before Christmas and it took us two days to get to Bellingham. We passed only one vehicle because we were going so slowly with the big load. The few places that were open were occupied by a lot of interesting ethnic people who weren't making a fuss about Christmas. We celebrated Christmas on the day after, and everything was good.

It was (of course) much colder in Bellingham. Rebecca's parents, Ruth and Paul Broward, had built their house just outside Bellingham a few years earlier. It was on windy sand spit, appropriately called Sandy Point, that got less rain than much of the area, but more wind, often gusting over 100 mph in the winter. However, the summers were usually sunny and warm there, and the crabbing was really good. Rebecca's father Paul was an engineer who had switched to construction work, which wasn't steady in the rainy northwest. At the time, Ruth and Paul had actually moved back to L.A. to work because the economy was slow in Bellingham, so they drove back to California after Christmas.

We moved into Rebecca's parents' house and shared it with Rebecca's brother Russell. Russell was keen on hunting, fishing, and his dog. He had moved to the area years earlier and loved the wide-open spaces. After cruising the wide open South Pacific with the family, L.A. didn't suit him, but the call of the Pacific Northwest did.

Relocating to Bellingham had several advantages. It's close to the Canadian border, which was important for us for accessing the Canadian health care system and for getting to Nuchatlitz. And it's a kayaking paradise, with dozens of islands to explore in the U.S. San Juans and the Canadian Gulf Islands.

I immediately rented an old warehouse known as the Carnation building, built about 100 years previously, used to make evaporated milk. The building was just minutes north of Bellingham, in the small town of Ferndale. The rent for the 4,000 square foot workspace was only $250 a month, but we first had to clean everything up. Our landlord was nice but a no-nonsense sort of fellow who appreciated that we had moved into a part of the building that was vacant. I joked that the place was so rundown even the street people had moved out. Before we took over the space, a company used it to render dogfish (small sand sharks), and we had to deal with a drum of shark oil they'd left behind. It was much easier to set up a business in the Ferndale area than in southern California, and the city was much easier to deal with in terms of regulations. Also our employees were from farms in the area and didn't mind hard work. The place took shape and we started building kayaks there on April 1, 1988.

Ocean Kayak Takes Off in Ferndale

Now that Ocean Kayak had a real home, progress began happening at an amazing rate. We started our growth curve of 30% a year. We hired Betty, who was a very professional secretary. Sandra Fussman was also one of our first hires; she could do anything. Our salesperson, Molly Rhodes, was fantastic for making deals with individual dealers, which we were getting by the week. We hired Del McAlpine, a CPA, although most people thought it was way too premature for that. It turned out to be a good move, however, because Del really grounded our procedures. Many Friday nights he would be there past 6:00 pm, making sure everything was in order. We were now a real company.

EIGHTEEN

A NEW HOUSE, A NEW BABY, A BOOMING BUSINESS

"Time is the only thing that keeps everything from happening all at once. Well sort of."

During the first six months of our work in Ferndale, we lived at Rebecca's parents' house. After spending time in Canada at Nuchatlitz, we liked being closer to a town. Before we moved north our do-everything-office-person, Sheila, who had done our bookkeeping, realized that she was taking more money out of the company than both Rebecca and I were. "How do you do it?" she asked us.

We lived so cheaply in the first six months in Washington, we had just enough to make a down payment, probably only about $6,000 to $8,000, on a small house in town. We found ours for $62,000. The real estate market had been flat in Bellingham for the last 10 years, and was about to explode. We had seen this happen in California but it was not a common event yet in the northwest. The house was brand new, but in an old funky Fairhaven neighborhood on the south side of Bellingham once called the Pit. Once the cheap hippie hangout of the 1970s, it was just starting to be the next hip place to live.

It was early July 1988, and Tristan was ready to be born. The deal on our new house was to close at the same time. On a Sunday afternoon, labor set in and I fretted about driving north through the border, for Tristan to be born in Canada, but we had no problem. At that time of year, that far north the sun starts lightening up the sky at 4:00 am, which was right around the hour Tristan was born. I went and got a coffee from a diner that had just opened. The waitress thought I had been out all night partying until I told her our son had just been born.

When we drove back across the border, the guard asked us if we had acquired anything in Canada, and we had to stifle our smiles when we said "No." The new house was very special to us. The neighborhood was very friendly. Although it was now part of Bellingham, Fairhaven had once been its own town, and had historic buildings and a wonderful bookstore that we could easily walk to. A little boat launch and even a small boat shop were about a block away.

Meanwhile, at Ocean Kayak, business was booming. Within a few years, there were many little small businesses near our factory in the same 100-year-old building. It had become the unassigned "incubator" for many companies that went on to grow. Bob, a guy upstairs in an adjacent building, was the second largest pottery wheel manufacturer in the world. Ocean Kayak took over more and more of the complex because the rent was cheap. For a while, we rented office space on Ferndale's Main Street, which we turned into a nursery for Tristan. Everything was new and exciting. Change was in the air.

Rebecca had been a journalism major. Her field was magazines and she had worked with her mother, Ruth, on several publications. Instead of creating a sales brochure for Ocean Kayak, someone came up with the idea of a tabloid type publication that would feature stories. For 10 cents apiece, we could have a paper twice the size of a brochure, with kayaking stories in it and a mention of our sit-on-top kayaks that made these adventures all possible. At less than ten percent of the cost of a brochure, printed in color and on nice paper, the "Ocean Kayak News" looked very professional. Paul Julian, who later worked as sales manager, told me that the way that Rebecca wrote these stories suggested that using our kayaks would be a lot of fun. She showed how we were a company that used our kayaks; we didn't just sell them to customers.

I think this was when we were beginning to see a switch in selling a kayak product vs. having the kayaking experience. Selling the product was secondary to having the experience. This is a much softer approach, Rebecca was a master at creating this new form of marketing, and it worked extremely well.

From the perspective of the customer, this had an interesting effect. They saw the glossy brochures from our competition, the Perception kayak company. Those brochures suggested we want your money and here is our product and we have to dress it up to look good with this expensive brochure. It was old school marketing. On the same table would be this adventure magazine that highlighted all sorts of fun outings. Ocean Kayak appeared to be the larger company even though at the time, we were only one tenth the size of The Perception Kayak Company, which was our competitor. We also printed an 800-phone number on our kayaks and in the Ocean Kayak News so people could call us directly.

Remember, this was at a time before cell phones or the Internet existed. Our phone number was easy to remember: 1-800-8kayaks. We were trying to be as accessible as possible so people

could make the decision and buy while they were hot on the idea. Later,

Paul Julian suggested that I put a small graphic of my name on the kayaks, which read, "Designed by Tim Niemier." I still get regular emails from that brand recognition.

Rebecca had a huge influence on the branding and development of Ocean Kayak. I think I can say that she was a pioneer in this new form of marketing. I don't think she ever got the recognition she deserved for her part in making Ocean Kayak what it became. Part of the reason she had such an influence was because she was a real water person. She had spent two years on a little sailboat traveling throughout Mexico, Tahiti, and Hawaii. The other part was that Rebecca really embraced the whole water friendly concept. She was able to put this magic experience down on paper in a professional way that outdid the marketing approach used by "Madison Avenue."

Selling Our Kayaks in California

Our first dealer in California was Mark Olson, from Santa Barbara, who owned Bike and Hike. He set the standard and raised the bar on what a kayak dealer could do. An older woman insisted that he get her one of our kayaks. He couldn't talk her out of it, so he became a dealer. He told us he wanted to be the only dealer in Santa Barbara, which had about 100,000 people. He sent us a deposit on 50 kayaks, and then proceeded to sell 114 of them the first year. I figured that is .001 or 1/10th of 1% of the population, which I noticed seemed to be the critical mass, which enabled sales of 100 to 200 every year.

Other companies began to sell the "sit-inside" kayaks in Santa Barbara. Those companies called our sit-on-top kayaks not "real" kayaks. So Mark coined the phrase "unreal kayaks" and became the rep for Southern California. I believe he worked for Ocean Kayak longer than anyone else, about the same amount of time that I worked for the company, from the time of my first sale to the day I sold it. Mark started as a dealer in 1986.

NINETEEN

THE BANZAI BOZOS AND THE ROCK GARDEN

"What happens to make a hero is the fact that they manage to survive."

I can't recall exactly how and when I ran into the group of kayakers who called themselves the "Banzai Bozos." The core group was Jim Kreoufski, Dave Nagel, and his brother, John Nagel. They lived just north of San Francisco. They were the main guys I paddled with when I visited California. They paddled the Marin and Sonoma coastlines, where there were a lot of rocks and also usually big surf. I think their original intention in forming the group was to harass another group from south of San Francisco who called themselves the Tsunami Rangers.

The Rangers consisted mainly of Michael Powers, Jim Kakook, Gordon Brown, and Eric Sores. The Rangers were well connected with video production and the media. Michael was a professional photographer and wrote articles about kayak adventures. I went on an expedition he

135

put together across the Altiplano, in the high Andes of South America. It was filmed for a half-hour TV show by Roger Brown, Gordon's father. The Rangers had their own kayaks, designed and built by Jim Kakook. They were fiberglass and prone to breaking. I don't think the Bozo's even owned a camera?

The activity both groups would partake in was called Rock Gardening: the art of paddling in surf around rocks. One slot was called Otis after the Otis Elevator Company, because the surf surged up and down 20 feet, but the slot was only 10 feet wide. We could paddle into some of the caves along the coast. After we were inside, a large set of waves could block the entrance, causing the cave interior to go dark and everyone's ears to pop. Headlights were required here. It was very exciting. The scene is really dynamic and seems completely insane, because when you see the waves explode as they crash on the rocks, it seems probable that a kayak would do the same thing, explode on the rocks. Quite the opposite is actually true. The waves act like a cushion and a paddler can keep his distance from the rocks except for the occasional scrape. There were a few injuries, but the thrill to injury ratio was pretty favorable. With wetsuits and helmets for protection, injuries don't happen that often. Kayaking like that is an inexpensive sport that can thrill you as much as base-jumping without the real danger of dying.

The Rangers had a comical but serious ranking to their members. They developed entertaining presentations, which they would deliver to the various sea kayak symposiums, representing themselves as the lunatic fringe of kayaking. Eric Sores was a marketing professor from Berkley who came off as a teenager who never grew up. He had incredible energy in these speaking engagements. The combination of the incredible photos of Michael Powers, videos from Gordon Brown, and the presence of Eric had people laughing and jaws dropping. I supported all this because they were using sit-on-top kayaks. Sea kayakers who were a whole other breed that generally stayed away from the rocks were the perfect audience. The Rangers even made some big TV slots in those days.

The Bozos, however, couldn't take a picture to save their lives, but they would go out and try to exceed the limits of whatever the Rangers had done. Dave Nagel had a high-stress job as a cop, and Jim Kreoufski did estimating for a construction firm, which was also stressful. They told me that the reason they did what they did was because when they were kayaking they were more worried about getting bashed up than worried about work. John Nagle was an ex-Navy Seal and usually ended up saving everyone. I gave them kayaks made from new polyethylene resins to test their toughness. The Bozos could eventually break anything, but the best resins would "rise to the surface" pretty quickly. Sometimes the bows would cave in or get big holes in them in the middle of one of their trips so they would repair them right there, with sponges or propane torches or even some epoxy putty.

The two groups maintained a friendly rivalry with the Bozos continually trying to embarrass the Rangers. During one kayak symposium, it was really hot just before the Rangers' presentation, and everyone took a break. During the break, one of the Bozos switched the VCR tape (remember those?) with one of Dave Nagel in a Bozo mask doing an interview while driving. (I took the video with my home video camera.) It took the Rangers five minutes to find the tape and replace it with their own. This was true Bozo piracy at work. I loved it.

Looking back on those times we all created, I feel incredibly fortunate to have been there. What was unique about the experience was that it gave us a lot of the camaraderie of going into battle, because playing in surf around the rocks was scary and thrilling but only a little dangerous. Trusting your group was crucial. The noise was so great that hand signals were the only way to communicate. Eric's explanations of what the various signals meant were hilarious.

We were playing in Nature without damaging the ecosystem. In Dave Nagle's old VW van, we didn't even use much fuel to get there. If kayaking is like immersing oneself in the "soup" of life, then Rock Gardening is like jumping into Nature's washing machine.

TWENTY

OCEAN KAYAK GOES TO THE NEXT LEVEL

*"Being around extraordinary people
can create an extraordinary team."*

In the fall, our area of the Pacific Northwest would sometimes experience a spate of warm rain just after the first early snow of the season. This was known as a pineapple express because the storm started near Hawaii. The warm rain would melt all the new snow on the ground and make the river rise. One day I had taken my four-year-old son into the factory on a rainy weekend. After a few hours I realized that the river had risen to the point that I could no longer drive out. I parked the car on higher ground and walked out but did have to get my feet a little wet at one point through water that was ice cold from the melting snow further upstream. Our offices came within one foot of getting flooded, but luckily stayed dry. In one three-year period, we had two of what they called "hundred year floods."

Ocean Kayak had the age-old tensions between Sales and Production Departments. Every year when summer finally hit the nation, everyone wanted kayaks yesterday. Then we struggled to build 100 kayaks a week with one machine and one mold. 100 seemed to be the magic number. Production was never happy when they had to suddenly start making more kayaks.

The Sales Department (actually just one guy) said, "Why should I try to sell more kayaks if production can't make them?" When production made more than were ordered, they would say, "Why should we make more kayaks if sales can't sell them?"

One week, I came up with a plan. If Production could make 101 or more kayaks that week, then the entire sales team of one guy and I would moon Main Street. Our factory was right on a main road and the small downtown area of Ferndale was just two blocks away, across the river. If Sales shipped 99 or fewer kayaks, then I, and the entire production team of five, would do the mooning.

So what was the number of kayaks made and shipped that week? Exactly 100. Main Street (and my own butt) was safe.

Olympic Champion Greg Barton Comes to Work for Us

In 1984 the Olympics were in Seoul, South Korea. A member of the flat-water kayak team was named Greg Barton. His nickname was Buck. Greg was from Michigan and won gold in the single kayak race by mere inches, then 90 minutes later won gold in the doubles with Norman Bellingham by at least six inches. I thought it would be wonderful if he worked for us. It turned out he had an engineering degree and had scored a perfect score on his college entrance exams. I made him an offer. People thought we were nuts because, at our rate of growth, it was already hard to keep up with payroll.

Hiring Greg was one of the best things we ever did. He lent a level of credibility and professionalism to our company that no other kayak company could even come close to. Everyone in our company started acting like a champion on a mission. Greg used these little day planners because he said after the Olympics his life got much more complicated and hard to track. Many employees at Ocean Kayak started using planners. He made me aware of how much effort an athlete puts into his work and how little most athletes get back from society in return. In Eastern Europe, in places like Hungary where flat water kayaking is big, Greg is a hero. Hungary's kayak team budget was greater than that of the U.S. canoe and kayak teams budgets combined.

During this time, I made a commitment to donate 100 trainer kayaks to the Atlanta junior team. If our Olympic or national team helped my business, I would help them. The U.S. hasn't had a champion like Greg since and he remained extremely competitive for decades after the Olympics. Now Greg and paddling Champion from South Africa, Oscar Chalupski, own Epic surf skis.

Working with Paul Julian

Another person I actually sought out was Paul Julian who did a great job for O'Brien Sailboards in Washington State. Paul had taught scuba, had a shop, and knew how to make it all work. He also knew how to set up a team of reps to sell to different areas of the U.S. as well as internationally. At that time, Paul knew that the sailboard market was collapsing and the sit-on-top kayak was a reasonably easy transition. We got our reps mostly from the sailboard industry; this set us apart from all of the regular kayak companies.

At that time we decided to expand into having reps sell the kayaks to dealers. We paid the reps 7%, but with this direct involvement of someone knocking on the dealer's door, we could expand our business and get the dealers we wanted, those who ordered over 100 kayaks a year. Paul had a lot of contact with the imploding sailboard industry. There were a lot of reps and dealers hungry for a similar product to sell. Our sit-on-top kayaks fit the bill perfectly because they looked sexy like surfboards but with almost no learning curve to master paddling them. In six months we had 12 reps, including an international guy, expanding our empire. This meant giving up margin or profit that we had to make up in volume, but it seemed to be working. We were growing like crazy. I never in my wildest dreams thought that my sit on top kayak would overtake the sailboard market.

We Move the Factory to Custer

Growth forced us to move. Ocean Kayak had taken over much of the Carnation building and still needed more space.

We had

started with the 14-foot all around Scupper, and then came out with the Scrambler, which was a smaller 11-foot long kayak that had a completely different look to it and didn't have the large hatches. It could be made with no hatches at all.

143

After that came the Frenzy and the Scupper Pro. We also had a double called the Zuma, which we later changed to the Zest because there was a sailboat called Zuma, and that company had more money for attorneys. We realized that we could not produce enough kayaks to meet next year's sales in the space we had at our Ferndale facility. We had to move.

There weren't many buildings around that met our requirements. We looked at building a place at a different location in Ferndale, but the regulations were tough. Then we looked at converting a building right in downtown Bellingham. That got complicated so we took a few drives to see if we could find something. Custer, just a bit further north of Ferndale, had an industrial park with a building about the right size, full of woodworking equipment and an empty parking lot during the week.

We went up to the main office and asked the owner if he wanted to sell the building. He said "$400,000." We said, "Sold." It didn't take much longer than that. No real estate agents and their fees. We ended up putting about $150,000 into newer offices and a pit for the oven. I didn't want to invest that much money into a place I rented. We were back in business in a "real" building.

Manufacturing in the Wild

Northern Washington is still a pretty wild place. The Custer industrial park had trees around the perimeter but not many trees within the park itself. Trees surrounded a small pond nearby that was there in case the fire department needed water. We used that pond, dropping kayaks in the water. I noticed one day that a few of the trees were cut down. Who would go and do a thing like that? On closer inspection, I saw gnawing marks. A beaver was responsible. When we were at the Ferndale plant, Sandra Fussman came in one day and said, "I think I saw a moose from the highway." She doubted herself because the weather was sort of foggy. Later she found out she wasn't imagining things as there had been a moose reported in the area. We never knew what might show up.

TWENTY-ONE

EXPANDING TO MULTIPLE KAYAK MODELS

"The way to make more kayak models to choose from is small models."

We loved our reps that sold our kayaks to our dealers and they loved us,

most of the time. When I came up with a new idea for a kayak, I would take an hour or so to make a little model. Then I would take the models to the Outdoor Retailer Show to pass around to all the reps that would sell to the dealers. When the reps held the 1/6 scale models in their hands the kayaks would seem much more "real" than any drawing. The models were carved from Styrofoam and about 2 to 3 feet long. I would then gather the models back up and hold one of them up and ask all of them, "How much should this model sell for?"

After going through a few models, I would come back to the first one and ask, "At that price, how many are we going to sell of this model?" I didn't keep track of who said what but just the end result. The reps now owned the outcome and at the end of the year the numbers were pretty close to their predictions. It was a simple and effective way to forecast sales by asking the very people who did the selling. One time we invited all of the reps to our factory to show our appreciation for them. Some of them said this was the first company who did that and the process really solidified our team.

The Scupper Original

Many people still say this design was the best overall sit-on-top ever because, at 14 feet, it was fast but not too long, and small enough over all to be lightweight. Scuppers weighed only about 43 pounds. Compared to other kayaks that are big and heavy, it was a winner. The Scupper Original really made Ocean Kayak because it was like a Volks-kayak in that it was for anyone and everyone. From the beginning, this one model sold in greater numbers than any of the Perception kayak company's individual models, which got the attention of Perception owner Bill Masters and made him rethink whether kayaks have to be specialized or general purpose.

The first rendition of the Scupper had the hatches front and back. For a long time we put foam under the seat to support that part of the kayak, but later we put scuppers in the seat and it worked better and was less work to make. When we switched to the second set of scuppers under the seat I worried that the boat would stick on the mold if it cooled too much, so we would pull the boat out when it was still pretty hot.

These Scuppers could be bent in half and would flex back and look almost the same and would paddle the same. The original Banzai Bozos used these kayaks for their "rock gardening" adventures and would break just about any type of polyethylene I would have them test. No one else would abuse them like the Bozos.

The Scrambler

The Scrambler was my attempt to make a smaller, lighter, and less expensive kayak to please even more people. The idea was that it

could be sold all stripped down or with smaller round 8-inch diameter pop-off hatches that could even be put in by the dealers. The Scrambler had a well in the back where someone could carry a scuba tank or whatever else they might want. It was small at only 11 feet long, fairly narrow, and weighed only 39 pounds. I put a bunch of scuppers in it, which made it strong enough to stand in when it was positioned like a beam on two sawhorses.

The center went through the water and the sides were a bit like surfboard sides that would conform to the natural flow of the water but add a little lift that you could feel when it would take off on a wave. The seat was fairly high, compared to the position of the foot wells, which made it comfortable to paddle. It was fairly fast for a short little kayak, perfect for anyone to use. We put eyelets on the sides so that straps could be attached that would go around the paddler's knees for more serious surfing. These straps would lock the kayaker in so the kayak could be leaned way over in the waves to turn. The side rails were curved, which would grip the water and turn the kayak in slow gentle curves. The whole look and feel was another step in a different direction in a kayak for everyone.

These kayaks stacked. Some dealers liked that because they saved floor space and they started selling lots of them.

The Frenzy

I named my next model the Frenzy, because I had to rush to get it done for the next sales season. I made both the Scrambler and the Frenzy from blocks of Styrofoam and long sanded boards to get really nice curves. This was my favorite part of the whole process because it was similar to making sculptures. I would fiberglass them with epoxy resin, which is a little more toxic than the stinky fiberglass resin, but the only kind that works well with Styrofoam. I wore gloves and other protective gear. Then I applied auto body filler and smoothed them out. It was a huge amount of work. I wasn't sure what type of tail would work, so I made half of the prototype one way and the other half the other way and took it out to the coast, a four-hour drive, to test it. After that, I made the next master, called the "Plug," about 5% bigger to allow for the shrinkage of the polyethylene.

There was a big conference for rotomolders in Chicago in the fall and I had an idea to take the model we called the "Plug" to the molders who would be attending the conference. I thought, why not  take it on the plane with me rather than putting it on some truck that could take weeks to get there and it might be lost or damaged on the way. The airline is faster and I thought they would take better care of it. I finished that morning and left with very little time to spare, so I pulled up to the outside baggage check-in at the airport and gave the attendant some money and told him I would give him more if it actually got there with no damage. It arrived with me and we both made it to the conference and the mold was done for the next season.

The Frenzy was only nine feet long, and wider, which made it incredibly stable. It was a shorter, fatter Scrambler. It was a little slower than the Scrambler, but fun to play with in the surf. It was big and wide enough that, by using the knee straps, I could just lean back when I was facing a huge wave that had already broken, with a six-to-eight foot tall wall of pretty angry white water coming at me. The Frenzy would jump right up on top of all the white water. This little boat could slip around on the waves, but was designed to go in a straight line, which a lot of little short kayaks usually don't do all that well.

A neighbor of mine in Bellingham, Fred Tanner, spends over half the year in Costa Rica, and likes to take tourists out in the Frenzy because anyone can easily paddle it. It's also easy to handle out of the water, haul on a trailer or a car, and easy to move to and from the water. He took me down a river in Costa Rica using the Frenzy. He pointed out a large caiman or crocodile on the shore, but said he'd never had a problem with the snappers even though the tourists didn't always stay in their kayaks.

The Banzai Bozos used the Frenzy around the rock gardens they liked to play in. With the Scupper Original, their motto was that timing was everything, because the Scupper was fast enough to make it through different passages. The Frenzy was stable enough that speed wasn't as important because the boat could muscle through slowly. The Bozos hung out on the coastline north of San Francisco. Great white sharks also like to hang out there, because it's near the seal rookeries and their favorite food. There were a bunch of kayakers around the town of Jenner, at the mouth of the Russian River, where a large bunch of seals congregated.

One day there, a woman paddled away from her group and a great white shark bit her kayak with such force that it damaged the kayak and threw her out of the boat. She was mostly embarrassed. She originally believed she had run into a rock, so she stepped on the rock to get back into her kayak. She was shocked to discover there was no rock; she had stepped on the shark!

That wasn't the first time it had happened but it was funny (to me anyway) that the name of the kayak she was using was the Frenzy. I kept that shark-bitten kayak around the shop to show my production employees that peoples' lives depended on the work they did.

The Zuma Two or Zest Two

The Zuma came about because we figured it was time to make a double kayak, so I took the Scrambler design and made it longer. These doubles worked well for companies who took people out on sightseeing trips,

like in Kauai. In Monterey Bay, tour companies used them to paddle out around the sea otters. At the time we were building the doubles, we had purchased boxes and boxes of little toggle pull handles for starting lawnmower-type motors. They became the perfect carry handles for the ends of the kayaks. They looked better than the PVC pipefittings that we used before that and they were a beautiful raspberry color. This color and the shape of the boats really attracted the sea otters in the Monterrey area. The otters would swim up and chew on the handles, much to the amazement of the paddlers in the kayak! For the tour companies, it was nice to have a double kayak to take the tourist who wanted someone else to paddle.

The Scupper Pro

I designed the original Scupper, which became the Scupper Classic, to hold some gear. So I thought, why not make a model that hauls even more gear for scuba divers and fishermen. The hatches of the Scupper Pro were quite a bit bigger than the Scupper Classic, with a different gasket system. The Pro was about the same width as the first Scupper, but about a foot  longer and 10 pounds heavier. This made the boat just long enough to need a rudder. With this model, and most all the models, we would blow air into the molds as they cooled to give the boats a fuller shape.

The Scupper Pro is still very popular in Hawaii for fishing. They take kayak fishing pretty seriously there because the surf and the ocean can be rough. Making the Scupper Pro showed me how adding just a little length can make the craft into a whole different kayak.

TWENTY-TWO

PUSHING THE LIMITS OF SIT ON TOP KAYAK DESIGN

"Instead of competing in a defined kayak just redefine the market instead and surf the wave of sales."

The goal for the Scrambler XT was to build a bigger Scrambler for divers. The XT was 10 inches longer, 1 inch wider and about 10 lbs. heavier than The Scrambler. This kayak was more stable than the Scupper Classic and had a lower seat. I surfed the XT at the annual Santa Cruz Kayak Surf Festival. It did well in those waves, which is saying a lot for a kayak that was designed for hauling dive gear around.

Although I lived close to the shoreline in Bellingham, barrier islands protect the waters there. So to test the XT and all my other kayaks, I always took them out to the Washington Coast (a four-hour drive) to try them out in the big rolling waves of the "real ocean."

This kayak was also a favorite with divers and lifeguards because it was bigger and could carry dive gear or another person. A lifeguard told me he could quickly paddle out to a victim and then immediately perform mouth-to-mouth resuscitation from the kayak. Then he'd lay the victim in the front of the kayak. Any water the victim spit up would drain out the scuppers while the lifeguard paddled back to shore. In San Francisco, they put these boats on fire trucks for such emergencies.

The Yahoo

With the Yahoo, we wanted to make a statement and get into the whitewater arena. Whitewater paddlers consider themselves the "experts" of the kayak world because they have to be able to roll and navigate through dangerous whitewater. For this project, I hired Mike Baker. Mike had Polish blood like me, so we called ourselves the Pole brothers. Mike grew up in Wisconsin and did a lot of whitewater kayaking and whitewater canoeing (C1) on the East Coast. He also knew how to use epoxy resins with fiberglass layups. When he first came out to the Seattle area, he worked for John Abenhouse, who started Northwest Kayaks; a company that built sea kayaks.

We also hired Cindy Dupuey, who was a whitewater kayaker and had led tour operations in San Diego. Cindy taught me a simple roll that I can usually still remember to do. Both Mike and Cindy helped educate the whole staff on how to sell this new whitewater kayak.

I also employed Tom Johnson, who is my biggest mentor and hero. Among many other things, he designed the first rotomolded whitewater kayak with Elmer Good in Southern California, back in 1973. Tom was on the forefront of the paddling industry but was very open minded to the sit on top idea. Mike taught me about whitewater and designs I was unfamiliar with, having stuck to the ocean and surf world in California. It was a trick to create a design for a kayak to track straight with the round bottom that is required for whitewater. Some whitewater kayaks are a real pain to paddle on flat water because they keep spinning, swapping ends. As a test, we paddled our Yahoo prototypes down the Nooksack River in the winter, when the sides of the river were frozen.

The other feature we put into this kayak was a "knee tree," a patented element that stuck up between the paddler's knees and was used to "lock" the paddler into the kayak to brace and even roll. That feature worked very well. One of the first times I took the kayak out in the spring, I fell out of the kayak and then just pulled myself back in without having to go through the whole act of bailing out the boat after chasing it down river. I loved it. In the surf The Yahoo worked well, but the hull shape didn't carve very well because it was designed to slip through the water for whitewater paddling, instead of digging into the water like a sea kayak.

The Malibu Two

The Malibu Two was my attempt at getting a price point double kayak that would be only 12 feet long, compared to our Zuma 2, which was about 16 feet long. At the time, coming up with a shorter  double was important, because a few employees had left Ocean Kayak after trashing our computers and doing some other damage, and they had started another kayak company just down the freeway a few miles. I knew they were coming out with a small double kayak. We ended up suing that company for stealing intellectual property, but I wanted to make sure we had a far superior double kayak.

At first, I planned to make a sit-on-top canoe-like craft. Rebecca's mother Ruth, in charge of Sales and Marketing, pushed me to do more. I've always loved a challenge. The other factor in play at the time was that I had just started taking ADD medication, and some people claimed that would stifle my creativity. I lived up to the challenge and designed the Malibu Two, a kayak that was probably one of the most important kayaks we made, second only to the original Scupper.

What turned out to be the winning feature of the Malibu Two was that it was both a family boat and could be paddled by only one person. Having this be a "family" purchase meant many more would be sold.

Judging by all the copies and near copies, The Malibu Two was probably the most popular model sit-on-top ever. After Johnson Outdoors bought Ocean Kayak, the sales of this model went so high that Larry Schonemacher made a machine that had nine molds on it and ran 24/7 making just the one model! That one model was over half of Ocean Kayak's total production. This proved to be too much of a good thing because everyone in the industry took notice and copied it. This model was patented but the 10-year-old patent they had didn't hold up in court after they spent three million dollars defending it. They would have been better off spending the money on developing newer designs rather than trying to protect an old one forever. In short, the Malibu Two was a real winner for Ocean Kayak and the industry. This model may be the most popular sit-on-top kayak ever.

The Sprinter

Greg Barton, our Olympic champion employee, was designing different kayaks for speed. He created a fiberglass model called The Black Marlin. We decided to make that model from rotomolded polyethylene. I helped a little on some of the cosmetic lines, but the shape was all Greg's. It turned out to be a very fast boat and even on occasion would beat some fiberglass surf skis, although it didn't succeed as well in Hawaii. It didn't have the right shape to go in rougher ocean swells. It was, however, and probably still is the fastest rotomolded kayak.

It's funny how some things are so far ahead of their time that it takes a decade or so to realize it. Recently Greg Barton's Epic Kayaks have come out with a Sprinter-like kayak. He has created a whole new class of fast

sit-on-top kayaks called surf skis, which are typically narrow, light, fast, and expensive. Epic made one that was short and fatter but still quite fast, and, to everyone's surprise, became the biggest seller in their line

because you didn't have to be an expert to use it the first time.

The Yak Board

When I put together the Yak Board, I was not trying to design a kayak, but a board type of craft. At eight feet long and 29 inches wide, I figured it would fit in an elevator at a Hawaiian

high-rise hotel. It was light, under 40 pounds, and would easily get a paddler around. It could also be stored on a boat or in some cars. The price point was $299.

We figured if we could ever get below $200, we would have the "no nod" kayak, which means that for a family on a budget, if the guy brings a $500 purchase home without checking with his wife, there would probably be a serious discussion. If the purchase were $300, the discussion wouldn't be as serious; at $200, it might not happen at all. The Malibu was great because it retailed for around $650 but it was a "family" budget item, not his or hers. One person could also paddle it as a single kayak so it was both a family purchase and an individual purchase.

The Rapido

My hero Merv Larson developed a line of surf kayaks in the 1970s. Merv was on the 1976 Olympic Flat-water kayak team at Montreal, Canada. Merv showed films of surfing these wonderful sit-on-top surfing boards and the Australians, South Africans, and other Olympic kayakers went nuts and started using them, but the Americans on the West Coast weren't as impressed because the only "surfing" was "surf board" surfing. Merv got out of the business, but his buddy Mike Johnson continued to make them 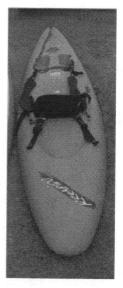 and compete with them at places like the Santa Cruz Kayak Surf Festival. Mike is the son of my biggest hero, Tom Johnson, who was one of the most influential people in paddle sports for many other reasons. Mike and I thought, what the heck, and we made the Rapido, a hollow polyethylene version of this great surf kayak shape. It worked quite well and would go much faster through surf sections than anything I had made for recreational paddling. I considered it a success and, after that, many other rotomolded kayak companies came out with real performance, surf-specific kayaks. These newer and surf-specific kayaks were ahead of their time. Later many companies started producing these few kayaks.

The Dawn Tracker and the Pocket Tracker

The Dawn Tracker and Pocket Tracker were created right around the time of the sale of Ocean Kayak. I didn't get to finish the concept, but it was to be an "in on top," which meant it was to be a hybrid that would be a sit-on-top with a spray skirt. We made an angled groove in the deck to lock down the spray skirt. The Pocket Tracker was to be a kayak that would handle well and fit in a small VW Rabbit car. The Dawn Tracker was designed to be the fastest kayak for its size, which was only 11 foot 6 inches long and 28 inches wide. This boat would cruise lightly loaded at a speed of about 4.5 mph, which is about what a sea kayak does. I say lightly loaded because most sea kayaks are never heavily loaded; they rarely go out overnight. It seemed wrong to have something designed to carry a two-week load then only take it on afternoon one-hour paddle trips. I took a Dawn Tracker out for a weekend and it performed well, even without a rudder.

The Cabo

The Cabo was a shape that I carved out in a scale model just before I sold Ocean Kayak. I am not sure who took on the project. I don't believe a full-size prototype was ever tested. I think they simply made the mold and went into production. The Cabo was intended to be a longer, faster, higher-volume and higher performance double for the sit-on-top touring companies. It was a bit narrow and a little tippy, but not as unstable as a surf ski.

Given a chance to paddle The Cabo in South America for a TV adventure travel program, I had to make a kayak that could be transformed into a catamaran to sail on rivers and lakes. The idea was to have a kayak that could go down the river, on the border between Peru and Bolivia that flowed into Lake Titicaca. I had to make the kayaks into catamarans by making cross arms that would fit across and attach to two kayaks. The whole contraption had to sail on a huge salt lake as well. All in all, The Cabo worked well for this project. The Cabo is a great cruiser kayak for this and other longer ventures.

TWENTY-THREE

WHAT HAPPENED TO ALL THESE KAYAKS
AFTER THE SALE?

*"Good judgment comes from experience;
experience comes from bad judgment."*

After the sale, most of the models except the Malibu Two, the Scrambler, and the Frenzy, faded. For the new owner, it was easier to sell more of a few models than continue to make new products and innovate in more areas and create more experiences on the water. There was innovation with the Venue, a kayak designed for women, and some innovations like the see-through port, but no major breakthroughs. Generally, after time, the fringe models that were pushing the envelope were dropped, and the middle-of-the-road models were pushed. Other smaller companies like Malibu Kayaks specialized and excelled in the fishing niche with specialty innovations.

The Evolution of Rotomolding Machines For Kayaks

Rotomolding was changing. There were still a lot of pioneer molders who built their own machines simply because there were not that many people who needed a machine that would just turn out kayaks. My first machine was the one I built myself in Malibu. It was pretty basic, but it worked for years as we produced the Scupper, which pretty much built the whole company. That single model sold more in its first years than any one of the 22 models that the larger Perception kayak company produced. This was a new business model, where one model of kayak could work for the majority of customers.

My first rotomolding machine cost me only a few thousand dollars to build. Machine number two was designed and built by Greg Barton and myself in the dead of winter. When we hired Greg, I realized that he was a very technical and calculating engineer, which was very different from my style of just designing something that looked good and wondering if it would break.

With our second kayak design, The Scrambler, we wanted to go with the same idea of one rotomolding machine for one kayak mold. Our second rotomolding machine was a much different machine than had ever been built or will ever be built, because it both heated and cooled the mold for the Scrambler and then we'd open the mold to unload and reload. I also wanted it to be cheap to build.

The idea was to have these molds lined up to build different models with one or two operators unloading the mold when the machine was done with its automatic cycle and loading it to produce the next kayak. The oven had to close tightly around the mold for efficiency, requiring very little heat although the cost of propane at the time was only about $2 to $3 dollars per heating cycle.

Greg and I literally did most of the building of the physical machine in an old warehouse in the winter. The building always seemed to be colder and damper inside than the freezing weather outside. We kept moving and wore insulated jumpsuits. Our meetings finished pretty quickly in that temperature. Greg and I worked well together. I would always push the limits and Greg would tell me how far we could go with the physical limitations of materials or design.

Rotomolding machine number three was a rig where we could put different molds into the bottom part of the oven, then lift that part up and seal it off enough to keep the heat in and still vent a bit. The idea with this one was to create one oven with a bunch of different carriages that could be loaded or unloaded. The lifting was required because we didn't have a pit for the molds to swing down into, so everything had to be up in the air. By this time we were getting more sophisticated with different computer systems that would run everything. When we to moved our operations from Ferndale to Custer, we had an opportunity to build new ovens. We had to dig a pit so the molds could roll in and out. The whole oven would tilt into the pit while the molds remained at floor level.

This oven system was actually two ovens; each was about 4x4x20 feet and would take two small molds or one big one. The molds would go on carriages, which were manually pushed in and out of the ovens. We had Bill Green design them and had the old Windsurfer production guys, Dave Phillips and Chris Ingram, build them for us. After we got these new ovens working, production could keep up with our growth for the next few years until we sold to Johnson Outdoors. On a side note, when the Ocean Kayak plant shut down in Washington State, the company didn't know what to do with the old ovens so they shipped them back to the New Zealand plant, which has now also shut down. I have faith that they will resurface once again in another chapter.

Saved by Jumper Cables

When large pieces of metal move around, static electricity will build up and when the molds come apart we could hear a big electric discharge. Greg had made a computer-controlled system to monitor and activate different things on the rotomolding machine. But when the molds opened, the electrical discharge would cause the computer to shut down. This was a real problem, because only Greg could fix the computer problems.

Finally my old friend Elmer Good visited us and showed us how to attach regular jumper cables to the mold before taking it apart. From then on, the cables worked perfectly to ground everything. The computer was fine.

Adding Graphics to Our Kayaks

We wanted a different look for all of our kayaks, so we put lots of graphics on them. The graphic designs were made by a company who started only a short distance away in Santa Paula, almost the same year as Ocean Kayak did, with the rotomolding era in 1986. The company, Mold In Graphics, grew at about the same rate as we did and even moved when we did, but they moved to Sedona, Arizona. After we put these graphics on our kayaks, our boats stood out from the others with the zingy designs. All the other kayak companies started buying graphics from Mold In Graphics.

Mike Stevenson started the company and later Mike hired Scott Saxman, who was and still is great to work with. Also they hired Jon Shriner, who used to make whitewater kayaks and then ovens, and now travels around with a motorhome like a nomad, visiting customers. They have a great company and enjoy what they do. They are part of my family. I asked them once how much business they got from my decision to put more graphics on our kayaks and they said, "Quite a lot." At trade shows, I don't mind having them take me out to dinner.

Mold In Graphics invented a way of making graphics for rotomolded products. They did this by taking a thin layer of colored polyethylene, the same material that the kayaks were made from, and putting it on a piece of paper that was like vellum. There was a little pad with ball

169

bearings in it and when the piece of paper was put against the mold and rubbed with the little pad, the graphic was applied. In the old days, if these graphics got below 50 degrees F they would flake off the paper and they would all be ruined. After this happened a few times, we designated a special graphics room that had its own heat just in case the main furnace went down. Nowadays the graphics are different and are not as temperamental.

Improving Our Cycle Time, Adding Up to Bigger Profits

Sometimes asking the right question is more important than sifting through masses of data. We upgraded our two rotomolding machines by increasing the circulating power of the fans that blew around the hot air. In this business, the time it takes to make the product, the "cycle time," is very important because the cost of the rest of the overhead is fixed. I asked how much money one minute of the cycle time would save us or cost us. It turned out to be about $6000 per week?

There were always a lot of numbers floating around our manufacturing process, but I believe I was the one to try to quantify how much our cycle time was worth to us. So many companies can't decide how to improve their process because of data overload. No one asks the right questions. The analysis gets even more complicated when you add in questions about perceived value from customers.

TWENTY-FOUR

SOMETIMES MIXING WORK AND FAMILY GOES WELL

"Almost everything in life is easier to get into than out of."

I put my mother-in-law, Ruth, in charge of Sales and Marketing. She was perfect for this period of our growth. She got us to the next level. Everyone warned me about hiring family members, but Ruth was a good fit at this critical time in our growth. Not only had she raised a family (an undervalued skill set in our society), but after her children were out of the house, she worked at a company that was probably bringing in between five and ten million dollars annually. She worked directly under the president as something between an executive secretary and a general vice president.

I wasn't aware of it then, but I probably wanted to prove to my own parents that I could be a success. However, by the time I was a success in business, my mother and father had both passed away. Maybe I was trying to get approval from my mother-in-law because both of my parents were gone.

In truth, Ruth was fun to work with and we worked well together. Ruth was truly amazing and her hidden talents grew wings. There are many women, especially stay-at-home moms, who don't realize how talented they are and neither does our society. In Ruth's case, her resume included sailing to Tahiti.

Ruth had valuable writing and people skills that were especially effective in getting out our message. She could also weed out any bad attitude that was brewing among our staff and make sure that everyone stayed on the same team. Ruth's mama-bear attitude was very helpful to unify the company in a stressful time of fast-paced growth. Ruth put everything into her job because she felt it was partly her baby too. Her department was upstairs, and it was all women. I considered hanging a "Save the Males" sign up there, but decided not to risk it. We had just hired an "HR" person.

Russ, Rebecca's brother, worked in production; I was amazed at what he would take on and accomplish. With all these talented folks on board, Ocean Kayak at that time was approaching five million dollars in annual sales.

And Sometimes Mixing Work and Family Is a Disaster

Someone told me that at five million annual sales, the perception among employees of preferential treatment for family members exists, whether the preferential treatment is present or not. When we reached this pivotal time, Rebecca and I hired a general manager who had run startup outdoor companies. It didn't work out. In a short time Ruth, Russ, and the General Manager were no longer with us.

As Sales Rocket and Competition Grows, We Decide to Sell Ocean Kayak

Before Ocean Kayak reached maximum growth, we had taken on some debt, which was another stress on our home life. The competition was growing. We knew we were going to sell the company eventually. As our sales grew and our home life soured, the urgency of selling became more real.

It became difficult for Rebecca and me to work together. We weren't living together. To help sell the company, we hired Matt Mullet who had been through a sale of a company and knew what was involved. Matt was strong on finances and had great accurate numbers from Del, who kept close track of all expenses and income from the very beginning of Ocean Kayak. Now all we needed was someone to buy us out.

We were fighting time, because we worried that Ocean Kayak was becoming vulnerable to all the competition that was starting to show up. We knew we didn't have the ability to make decisions if we were divided. We could not show weakness in this new sales environment at our level of sales. We could envision all of our success going down the drain if our family squabbles or an outside event caused us to implode.

We needed to sell the company soon. We didn't have much time to make that happen.

Reflections

As Ocean Kayak grew and I matured as a businessman, I realized that I didn't have to be good at everything. I only needed someone on the team who could do what I could not. With the support of great team members in my company, I felt like I could do anything. My ADD turned into a singular focus: designing and manufacturing kayaks. My passion for my company outweighed my fear of failure, and I was not afraid to tackle any challenge.

Nowadays I would say to anyone starting a company: Commit yourself to success and start your marathon. Like me, you'll figure out the rest along the way.

Stepping Up to Be the Leader

In Jung's archetypes, this is the King energy, the Visionary, the person who can envision something complete and communicate this vision to others. I was naturally a follower from my early years of being the second sibling, always looking up to my older brother.

I could finally use my ADD, which had previously been a distraction, to learn about all aspects of the company. Before leading a company, personal confrontations really bothered me. But now I understood that the welfare of the whole was much more important than the welfare of one individual who couldn't fit in.

Adding ADD Medications

When the company was really starting to rock, I decided to get on ADD meds. These drugs are basically amphetamines or speed, but very specific in what they do. I considered them to be less of a drug than coffee or, most certainly, alcohol. Prozac, combined with the ADD meds, gave me the ability to confront people in a way that I never had been able to do before. I could remain completely focused and not get jangled by someone yelling at me inches away from my face. I didn't back down and I didn't get angry or nervous. The meds gave me the power to be peacefully forceful compared to other drugs.

Decision Making Is Essential for High Growth

Making decisions is more the Warrior, or as I call it, the Hunter energy, the energy of setting boundaries and getting things done in a fair and businesslike way At Ocean Kayak, things were moving along pretty quickly and change was constant. There wasn't time to sit back and wonder which way to go. I found that when my back was up against the wall, I could make a very quick decision and move on.

Embracing My King Energy

Carl Jung describes this leadership energy as the "King energy." The King energy is a sort of bringing together of all the other energies. The King respects and honors all of the other energies because he has experienced all of them. Now he makes them all work together. He can paint the picture of the future so it is clear as day for others to follow.

In some ways, this episode in my life brought all my energies together. It was also very stressful, and, as strong as one can be with all the passion involved, there are little weaknesses that show up from constant stress. Sometimes, even if one can keep going, he may not want to. The Hunter always wants to find something new to hunt. What happens when the Hunter or the Visionary has to find something new to do and must go through a complete readjustment of his life? This was about to happen to me.

TWENTY-FIVE

THE SALE, FREE FALL, AND RECOVERY

"I felt like Faust selling Ocean Kayak.
It was like selling my soul but it had to be done."

This was a very stressful and lonely time. Anyone on the outside probably thought we should be happy. We were selling our company. We had a ton of emotions that we couldn't let go of, yet we had to move forward. The period after which we had decided to sell the company was hard for Rebecca and me. We had to work together even though we had so much to disagree about. I had moved out and was living in a little windswept marina on a small boat we had bought. I felt so alone. It was winter, and the icy wind whistled through the wooden boat. I felt like I had been exiled. When a marriage breaks up, why does the man always have to move out?

The Pre-Sales Process

There needs to be a whole process to selling a company. Your employees may start thinking that the buyer will immediately replace them with their own people and havoc can break loose and cause disaster before any sale takes place. The timing of our announcement was critical. Ruth was really good at managing that sort of process but she wasn't working at Ocean Kayak anymore.

We somehow managed to keep the staff on a positive note by saying that usually the buyer puts money into the company they purchase to supercharge it. Some of the things that needed to be done to make Ocean Kayak more saleable were sort of window dressing, but were a little hard to take. There were a lot of expenses that got attributed to R&D (Research and Development) to make it look like, once I was gone, the company could finally start making real money. I went along with that.

I was told that having less family remaining for the new owners to deal with was supposed to be beneficial, probably because they would view family as a liability, not an asset.

I Was No Longer Living in the Moment

Working at Ocean Kayak, while things seemed to be unraveling, was no longer very enjoyable. A lot of my buttons got pushed, because I was never very good at quantifying things on a spreadsheet. Luckily I didn't have to, because Matt Mullet and Del McAlpine were doing a great job at that. The process was largely out of my control, but going well. Maybe it was the lack of control that got to me. I was better at building up the business and not as good at getting ready to transfer it, even though I should have been happy about the sale. Maybe I felt anxious because I didn't know what would happen next.

Zodiac Was Interested; Hobie Cat Came Snooping

The Zodiac Company, that made inflatables and had purchased the Tahiti inflatable kayak company, was interested. The Hobie Cat Company did an official "we are very interested in buying your company tour" but was only trying to get as much information as possible. Soon after the tour they started their own Hobie Kayaks to prop up their Hobie Cat line that was losing popularity to boats that didn't require a trailer. We were polite and gave them minimum information.

I think Paul Julian tipped us off to what was going on through one of his many connections. Sometimes a customer might want to buy large numbers of kayaks and say the boats would be taken out of the country, but then they would end up in Costco for a discount price. This is called "gray marketing," because it really isn't illegal, just deceitful. Paul could easily spot one of these guys. Matt Mullet, who had taken over sales, wasn't as familiar and sold a ton of our kayaks to someone and they ended up in Costco. Luckily it didn't hurt our progress on selling the company. The dealers, however, did react, but that didn't seem to matter at this point. Finally the letter came.

Johnson Outdoors Makes the Offer

We learned later that Sam Johnson wanted to buy Ocean Kayak. He sent an offer then initiated a due diligence process. In our case, the process only took a few months but it can take six or more months to complete. Due diligence is the term used for the process when the purchasing company examines all the records and tries to find any, and I mean any, reason why they should not buy a company. This includes any aspect that could pose a risk to them after they acquire the company.

Matt would walk around with Del, who would shuffle tons of papers to show this and that. It seemed like before the last paper was found, there was another question about something else, requiring a new paper search. This went on for weeks. Fortunately, Del had kept impeccable records on everything, which made Matt's job easier.

After all was said and done, Johnson Outdoors personnel said they would like to start making a profit in three years or less. They also said that they wanted to keep all the current employees in place, which made our staff relax a little bit, but just a little. One thing that a speedy due diligence process does is cut down on a lot of the $300 dollar per hour lawyer time.

Sam told me that the main reason he wanted to buy Ocean Kayak was that many lakes across the U.S. were outlawing outboard motors because the lakes served as the drinking supply for the nearby communities. People would still want to get on the water and more people could get on the water more easily with our sit-on-top kayaks. It was about that simple. Sam could be very direct and in the end what he said was very important. This direct logic was sometimes completely overlooked by detail-oriented people. This information probably wouldn't be a part of any more formal due diligence process, but for us, it was probably the most important part. It took a leader like Sam, who could write the checks, to make the purchase happen quickly. This doesn't happen in many large companies with weak leadership.

Finally, we got to the sign-off on the last day of June 1997. The announcement went out July 1. There was a big picnic a few weeks later where Sam came out and spoke, and it gave most everyone a better feeling that their jobs were secure. Everything was pretty much the same and back to normal, at least for a while. Ten years later, on exactly the same day, almost to the hour, it was announced that Ocean Kayak was moving the entire manufacturing facility to Maine to join with Old Town Canoe because of sagging sales. The company had become a follower, not a leader.

What Was I Supposed to Do Now?

I was a little scared. As all the dust settled after the sale of Ocean Kayak, at first I was happy, but then it sunk in that my life would be very different from now on. I was pretty stressed. I was at my limit of my abilities. They'd taken me much further than I ever thought possible. I was glad I had "gone for it" with Ocean Kayak. I had proven to myself that I was smart enough and artistic enough to succeed in a big way. As part of the sale contract, I had to sign a seven-year non-compete agreement. After I regained consciousness, when the excitement of the sale was over, I felt like I had sold my soul to the devil. I had exchanged my passion for what I truly loved, designing watercraft, for money. The wording of my agreement sunk in: I couldn't make kayaks for a while and that was that.

I thought I would be able to stay on and do design, which I did for two years. It was sort of weird because I used to be the boss and now I wasn't. I tried to ask everyone which direction they wanted to go, rather than saying it had to be my way. We created a large fishing kayak called the Ambush. I thought the next growth area for paddlesports was in fishing because there are many more fishermen than kayakers and they are used to spending money. That is true to this day. The Ambush was too far ahead of its time. Now fishing is the main growth part of the kayak market. After the two years of consulting on design, the new owners felt that they could do what they had to do without me. I was glad the company was doing well. Of all the companies that Johnson owned, Ocean Kayak was the top producer and the most profitable.

TWENTY-SIX

FORMER BUSINESS RIVALS
BECOME PERSONAL FRIENDS

"The light at the end of the tunnel may be the oncoming train."

A friend and serious rival of mine, Bill Masters, sold his company, Perception Kayaks, at about the same time I sold Ocean Kayak. What made his situation rough was he really started the polyethylene kayak industry. He made this type of kayak popular throughout the world, mostly in whitewater kayaks.

Bill and I weren't competitors anymore. Even when we owned our companies, we had a lot of respect for what each other had accomplished. We also both suffered from the same post-sale "what do I do now" depression. With both of us, building our businesses had been such an all-consuming quest that when it stopped, we both were lost. We would call each other and try to make sense of it together.

People have told me that the three people that really changed kayaking were Bill Masters, John Dowd, and I. Bill introduced the sport to polyethylene, John Dowd introduced the sea kayak, and I introduced the sit-on-top kayak. Together, our efforts gave birth to the recreational kayak movement.

We all felt pushed out of the industry by people who thought they had "better ideas." But a little independence is good sometimes. I also believe that all three of us needed a break from the business world.

Breaking Up with Rebecca and Her Family

Before the sale of Ocean Kayak, I was miserable because Rebecca and I were separated but couldn't get a divorce until we sold the company. I felt very alone throughout this period because I had previously filled my life with Rebecca's family, which included a lot of rich relationships. I seemed to go from a perfect son-in-law to an outlaw almost overnight.

I finally knew what it felt like to be the dumpee rather than the dumper in a relationship. I also realized that as much as I would like to blame someone else, I had created the whole situation, including my relationship with the kids and all. I remember going to marriage counseling, where both Rebecca and I stubbornly clung to being "right." I often wonder if I knew then what I know now, about relationships and myself, would our marriage have fared any better? Or was this whole part of my life an unrealistic dependency that was unhealthy and couldn't have lasted anyway. Was this a time for me to be alone?

Exiled to Boat and Apartment

After Rebecca and I had separated, I was living on a boat in a marina 20 miles out of town. On windy, freezing winter nights, it was hard to heat up. The boat was a 36-foot-long wood-hulled trawler-type boat built locally at Friday Harbor in 1958 by a company that built fishing boats. This was one of only a few they built as pleasure boats. I did love the fact that I could untie it and get away to the nearby San Juan Islands on the weekends.

I really missed being around the kids and would get them only on the weekends. A while later I got an apartment nearby that had a dock where I could park the boat right in front so I could look at it. The kids and I would go out to the islands on adventures. One night there was a comet visible in the sky when I put them to bed in the boat at a scenic little cove. I will always remember that moment.

When I took the kids for the weekend, I would have to make four 20-mile trips between my apartment and Rebecca's house in town. I did not like that part of the arrangement. At this new apartment, I felt a sense of freedom, but I still missed having family life around me.

What Happened to Other Family Members at the Time of the Sale?

Russ went on to work for Ocean Kayak's main competition, Perception Kayaks. He did a great job at managing a division for them that created their first kayak for the mass market, sold in big box stores like Wal-Mart. Everyone knew this day was coming; we just didn't know who would do it first. The kayaks were made at a factory that made pipefittings and could make these kayaks for half the cost that Perception could.

While marketing for Mainstream Kayaks, Russ did everything himself, including selling to Costco and other big box stores. This was considered "selling out" by most the kayak manufacturers. We knew someone would eventually do it but none of us wanted to be the first. I always regret not being able to keep Russ at Ocean Kayak, because he may have been able to do something similar for us. After the company sold, Rebecca and I finalized all the court business that ended our marriage. I was officially out of that family, going from in-law to outlaw. We did realize that we would still be a family for the rest of our lives, so we were adult enough to not complain about each other in front of the kids. I eventually got over my feeling of abandonment and accepted the feeling of independence that I had never quite felt before.

Family Life after Divorce

After the divorce, I read a lot of books that helped me to analyze what had gone wrong with my marriage and me. I realized how little most people, including me, know about certain dynamics. It was an eye-opening experience to realize how something like birth order can affect your attraction to a spouse. I was the younger of two brothers, while Rebecca was the older sister of brothers, so our relationship had a familiar "fit" to our families of origin. At home with my parents and brother, I grew up fairly independent. When I got married and lived in

California, I shared a lot of the same friends with Rebecca's family. My family didn't have nearly the network of friends they did, especially ones that were involved with boats and the ocean. After moving to Washington State, I buried myself in work. I felt pretty alone when I was not working. At first, I missed the lifelong friends I had in California. Eventually I developed some relationships in Washington that later blossomed into great friendships.

I finally started appreciating being independent again like I had been while growing up. The big difference was that now I had self-confidence and no older brother telling me what to do. I started feeling really great.

I wondered why I always felt like a second-class parent. After the sale, I had time to be an equal parent. I didn't mind the child-support payments, but really wanted equal time with my kids. I finally read an article in Newsweek that explained that women run into the "glass ceiling" at work and men run into the "estrogen ceiling" at home. If a man is taking care of his kids, people often say things like "Are you being the mom today?" But maybe most men don't want to be equal parents and are happy to spend less time with their children. It was hard to accept this second-class-parent business, but it made me painfully aware of others in the same position. This fact has not changed much in the last 20 years.

The kids and I had many adventures together. We skied and snowboarded. Tristan and I were in the Scouts. We had a great Scout group that was very active. Tristan was with the same group for his whole scouting career. We went to great places like New Mexico. To this day, I think Tristan is unusual for his generation in the way he likes the outdoors instead of being consumed with a lot of electronic gadgets. My daughter Hannah is talented with her hands in making artistic things like I did at her age. She has a real eye for style. She also rose to a very high level in dance, which I salute because it is both artistic and athletic. Hannah is very driven and determined to excel.

Tristan enjoys climbing and leading groups in roped single pitch "routes" up rock faces. I think he shares my joy at seeing other people do what once scared them. His clients often want him to take them on trips the next year because they felt so safe with him and had a memorable experience. I am very proud of both my kids and look forward to a lifetime of great experiences with them while respecting their independence.

TWENTY-SEVEN

FINDING MYSELF AGAIN

"I never knew where I was or who I was till I moved and was moved."

The day after we sold Ocean Kayak, I closed on a new house near the lake in Bellingham. It had a great big shop. This was really a new beginning for me because I could make my house into whatever I wanted it to be. The shop was perfect for incubating new kayaks and other boats, which is what I really wanted to do again. In so many ways, life was shaping up to be perfect in my little nest within a community I really enjoyed.

I enjoyed being the sole owner of my house. I did a big remodel on it because it only had one spare bedroom and I had two kids. Tristan and Hannah each needed their own bedroom. I designed the remodel so the new bedrooms for Tristan and Hannah were well designed. I let the kids choose which one they wanted as well as their colors, which remain the same today.

This was the first time I remodeled a house for me alone. It was really nice to make all the decisions. I opted for colors in a feng shui style and added two larger bedrooms that could be converted into a rental unit after the kids moved out.

With all the remodels going on, I didn't have time to use or maintain the dear old trawler-style boat, so I sold it. I was back on solid ground in a big house. It gave me the sense of security I needed at that time. I created my own space my own way for the first time in my life.

Going to Nuchatlitz After the Sale

Nuchatlitz is my sort of rock in my life. It has been the one thing that is always there like a temple for me to go back to. It has been part of every aspect of my adult life. I ended up keeping Nuchatlitz after the divorce. Rebecca had no interest in it and selling it would have been a hassle, so I ended up with it after the divorce.

All through the years of my focus on growing Ocean Kayak, it was hard to get to Nuchatlitz. Now I had a chance to get back up there and really enjoy it. I took the time to do the finishing touches that I had always wanted to do. I remodeled the kitchen just the way I liked.

I gave Rebecca one of Girl Nan's baskets and I fixed up Stuart's old rowboat for her because Rebecca had a house on the lake and could use it there. I decided to get rid of everything that I didn't need at Nuchatlitz and either took it home or burned it in a big ritualistic fire. That experience was very cleansing. I felt like I was ready to start fresh.

My Daughter and I Travel to the Galapagos Islands

I wanted to do something special with my daughter. She wouldn't be at home for much longer. A good friend, Eric Ludwig, had contacted me to see if I was interested in going to the Galapagos Islands with him and his kids. I thought this would be a perfect Dad-Daughter trip. Eric was an ER Doctor from Juno, Alaska who had two daughters, one a little older than Hannah. The others on this proposed trip were almost all from the medical field. Rebecca, being protective, was hesitant and asked, "What if something happens?" I told her we would be well prepared with two ER doctors, a nurse, and even a shrink, so she agreed. The best part was the kids all together, because normally only older people end up traveling to the Galapagos.

Hannah and I flew to Ecuador's capital, Quito, a little early and found a woman from Argentina who had horse trips for the day up to various volcanoes. We saddled up. Hannah and I knew what we were doing because we had taken riding lessons together. During most of our lessons, we had trotted. These Ecuadorian horses liked to gallop up the wide-open trail, which was a thrill. We stayed in a magical place in town called Cafe Cultura, which had fascinating murals on all the walls.

There were other interesting travelers who stayed there and it left both of us with great memories. Then we joined up with the rest of the crew and spent some time in Quito. I still remember the Latin hot chocolate that only cost about 15 cents. We took a plane out to the Galapagos Islands and got on this really great motor-sailer that looked very seaworthy. For the next week and a half, it was our home. I had packed one of the first crude digital cameras.

The crew had young guides who told us all about why the animals in the islands never had the predators that most other places have. Without predators, the animals are totally unafraid of humans. We were there in the winter, which on the equator doesn't really affect the weather. It was a great time to visit, because so many unusual birds were nesting at that time of year. This was the first time that Hannah was the top dog in a pack of kids. When the other little girl was asked whether she wanted waffles or pancakes, she'd respond, "What is Hannah having? I will have what she has." It was a great time for Hannah to feel special, and not be just the younger sister. Helping me get out of the younger sibling mode was a gift that other adults gave me when I was Hannah's age, and I really appreciated it. The animals in the Galapagos were spectacular and I took photos with my little camera. After dinner I would look at the pictures and sketch them. Birds are hard to capture in a sketch because they generally fly away long before you can draw them. This was a very special trip.

TWENTY-EIGHT

BOATING IN BOLIVIA

"Let the adventures begin from outside and within."

During my non-compete period, I still wanted to make some sort of craft that would go on the water. Michael Powers of the Tsunami Rangers often went on trips as the photographer; he did a lot of world traveling on the cheap. A friend of Michael's wanted to do a half hour TV show on traversing the Bolivian Altiplano, the high plateau between Bolivia and Peru in the Andes.

Roger Brown produced these types of shows and had an idea for traveling from Lake Titicaca to the Uyuni Salt flats in Bolivia in self-propelled craft. They needed a vehicle to convert from a kayak to a catamaran and sail both on land and water. I like that sort of challenge. I took two Cabo double Ocean kayaks because I knew there was already a dealer in Santiago, Chile, not too far from Bolivia. I called Ocean Kayak and they hooked me up with the dealer and I convinced them to put four Cabos in their next container.

Then I welded up some cross members that bolted to two Cabos with a place to mount a sail to plug. At the time Johnson was making a little sailboat called the Escape that had the perfect sail. I worked pretty hard and assembled everything but hadn't tested my rigs out yet. Michael showed up and looked at everything then called Roger and said, "Yeah, it looks like it will work."

A day or so later, Roger showed up with Arlene Burns, who is a kayaker with a lot of first descents down really big rivers around the world. We took the catamaran down to the lake and luckily it was blowing hard enough to make the craft go way faster than we could paddle. None of us had ever gone that fast in a kayak and without even paddling. The trip was on. I learned later that Roger had sent Michael up as a scout to see if I was for real.

194

When we got to Bolivia, they were having a countrywide strike. One faction blocked all the roads to protest a large corporation trying to take water rights away from everyone (even the rights to rain water). After a few days, the matter was settled. The strikers won and got their water rights. Bolivia now has a liberal native person running the country. We got on the road to start filming. Since some of the people that were part of the show couldn't be there at certain times, we did the trip out of order, but it all came together in the end. All this time we were living at about 12,000 feet in altitude. One of the guys on the trip had a soccer ball, which we would knock around. We quickly got out of breath, especially when the ball went out of bounds. Soon the ball owner realized he should have taken a few more balls, because our soccer ball was eyed with great envy by all the locals.

We had to drive to a little port city at the far north of Chile, where we picked up the four Cabo kayaks to make two catamarans. The border between Chile and Bolivia was at 15,000 feet. Then we had to drive downhill forever. Back at camp, I assembled everything and we were off down the river. Camping at altitude was frosty at night, although we were right on the equator. Days were mild and always clear because hardly any moisture makes it past the Andes western ridge. Having a woman along (Arlene Burns) who did a lot of the talking for the program was good, because it kept the humor level to a certain standard and made evening conversations more interesting. Everyone on the trip had enjoyed many adventures and now we finally had a lot of time to hear them all.

We used the sails going down the river that linked Lake Titicaca to the Uyuni Salt Flats. This drainage system floods huge areas with only a few inches of water at certain times of the year. We passed a muddy gathering place for tens of thousands of flamingos, which, I was surprised to discover, were common at such a high elevation. Eventually the floodwater evaporates, leaving behind a very minute amount of salt. The salt built up over millions of years and is now hundreds of feet

thick. The salt flats were eerie. They looked like a big white ocean with rocky islands here and there. The wind was supposed to blow really hard there, and at first we thought the sails might be too large. However, when the wheels went down and the steering was hooked up, we had no wind. We camped there for several days and on only one afternoon was there enough wind to go a few hundred yards.

Then we were off to Lake Titicaca, which is the highest large lake in the world. The native kids invaded our camp, speaking a language that was not Spanish. We were told that computer language was derived from their native tongue because it was more logical than just about any other language. I really enjoyed how free and unrestricted the kids seemed, while still being respectful.

We met up with an American archeologist who had made some great discoveries in the area. There was evidence of the Incas, who built precise canals to transport water from the high snowy peaks down to their cities. The water system in ancient Inca times was very advanced and supported more people than were living there when we visited. However, the Incas were sort of like the Romans or Americans in that they brutally invaded and then dominated all the local tribes. When the Spanish arrived, the Inca nation fell. According to the archeologist, the islands we visited were sites where the virgin girls were sacrificed to the gods. The islands reminded me of California's Channel Islands, but smaller, with fresh lake water surrounding them. One of the locations where sacred items had been found was just offshore, right at the surface of the lake. When Arlene stood on the rock there, on film it appeared like she was walking on water. This was the sort of adventure that I wanted to do more of.

TWENTY-NINE
MEETING THE LAST MASTER NAVIGATOR
IN MICRONESIA

"I believe therefore I sea."

Another adventure opportunity presented itself, this time in the South Pacific, in Micronesia. Steve Kasperbauer rented most of the kayaks in Guam, just south of Japan. Guam is an American territory, sort of like Puerto Rico. For Asia, Guam is similar to Hawaii in that it is only one time zone away and a popular place to get married or take the traditional holiday between school and a lifetime of work.

For all these tourists, Steve designed a one-hour activity package that included kayaking, jet skiing and going up in a hang glider-like apparatus. What a bargain! The kayaking portion lasted 20 minutes but gave everyone a taste of that experience. I asked Steve how many people took his package tour every year. His answer: over a million. This had been going on for decades, so that was the basis for my billion butts in boats concept. Here were 30 million on one island that was only about 20 miles long. The guys who worked for Steve were from the islands where the last outrigger navigator who could navigate without compasses still lives. They were ordaining a priest on the island where the grand navigator lived. I had to go.

I got a fantastic camera guy, Chris Emerick, to come along. He also knew

Arlene Burns and tried to get her to go but didn't succeed. I wanted to film this event. Chris had done a lot of action kayak videos. After a long flight through Japan and Guam, we arrived at Saipan, one of the islands that were among the first that the Japanese took over. Intense fighting took place here at the end of the war. My father served in the Army in this general location. Some Japanese soldiers believed it was not honorable to surrender and were discovered as late as the 1970s hiding out even on Guam, over 20 years after the end of the war.

In Saipan, we couldn't help noticing that some of the women wore only a lava lava skirt. They weren't the least bit embarrassed to be bare-breasted; we quickly realized that it was entirely our hang-up. After a day or so, we boarded an old 200-foot ship, the Micro Spirit. The passengers were all native people except for about five white guys. One of these was from Seattle and another guy, Frank Culp, lived about 15 miles from Bellingham. I couldn't believe it. Frank had been going down there for years and even sponsored some kids to go to school in Bellingham. Some of those kids and others still live with him in Bellingham.

The Micro Spirit was very crowded. We slept on pads on top of pallets to stay out of the water that ran across the deck from the rain. The temperature was hot and humid at about 90 to 100 degrees Fahrenheit. It didn't seem overly hot, but it was impossible to ever get chilled or even cool. We were on this ship for about a week, weaving our way through the different islands until we got to our destination island, Satawal, which is less than a mile long. These islands were the real South Pacific. Little palm trees, sandy spits, and classic coral atolls.

The Micro Spirit was a noisy old transport vessel. There was no food service on board, and we had brought only about a week's worth of food. There were pigs on board going to and from different islands, and because it was the end of the school year, some kids were going back home. I didn't know what to expect, but I was delighted at the friendliness of everyone. The first phrase we had to learn was "I am full," because everyone wanted to share their food with us. We didn't know what we were eating; often it was turtle or fish wrapped up in a woven palm frond basket. There was little imported food except for dried Japanese noodle soups. As we got further away from civilization into the outer islands, everyone got even friendlier. Most of the women wore only skirts. I learned that covering up the thighs for a woman here was like western women covering their breasts. Many of the men wore skirts, too, consisting of about three yards of material wrapped around their waists. At these temperatures, clothing was never needed for keeping in body heat. Much of the reason I wanted to go on this whole trip was to meet and talk to Mau Piailug, who was said to be the "last master navigator" able to navigate without a compass. With GPS technology widely available today, you might ask why it is important to honor these old methods. To me, it was honoring the amazing ability to be so in touch with the nature of the ocean. The earliest ocean voyagers knew there is so much more to being on the water than seeing yourself as a blip on a computer screen. On board with us was Allen Rosen from L.A., who was doing his own documentary on Mau. We all slept on the deck, while Mau occupied one of the three or so staterooms.

202

Mau had years ago gone to Hawaii to teach the Hawaiians the knowledge they had lost about ocean navigation and paddling canoes. In 1976, Mau had piloted the replica of a large sailing canoe named the Hokolaea from Hawaii to Tahiti with no compass. Even with overcast skies for the last three days of the trip, the big canoe arrived within a three-hour predicted window of time.

Mau told me there were seven ways to tell where you are: wind, current, feeling the wave action, clouds indicating an island even over the horizon, animal life such as birds, stars of course, and (I believe) weather. There is a ceremony for navigators called the Pwo ceremony where they have to remember not only how to get to islands but how to navigate through the tricky inlets in the coral reefs. The navigation is a lot of memorization, but also using little charts made from native materials as navigational aids. Navigators had a special place in Polynesian society because they had a lot of power when at sea, even rivaling the chiefs.

When we arrived at Satawal, 20-plus foot boats would transport us into knee-deep water and unload all the supplies. However, at Satawal the local people had seen us coming. They all lined up and started singing a welcoming song. Chris and I wanted to document this, but later we realized that they were singing just for us. It was really special.

I had been talking to a guy who told us that we would be sleeping at a relative's house. They gave us coconuts that were for drinking and didn't have much meat, but the liquid was healthy and refreshing. There were big thatched open buildings with canoes in them, some only for men and others only for women. Many activities seemed to be gender-specific. Many of the men, I learned, had degrees from universities in the U.S., and Oregon seemed to be the place many of them studied. After that, they came back here to their island homes. The outrigger canoes were called proas and were built to travel in either direction when they tacked. They were all wood. The smaller ones were carved out of one log; the larger ones were pieces tied together with coconut husk rope and another spongy material between the planks. They would sometimes use the foam from fishing floats instead of the native materials. I learned that the outriggers were still in use because fuel was very expensive and there were few jobs to generate money on the more remote islands.

More people arrived and were greeted as we were with songs. There were various groups that would perform different dances and songs from the surrounding islands, but all the festivities were to honor the ordaining  of a priest to Satawal. The religion there is Jesuit, but all the priests are locals, without dress codes like the Catholics imposed on the natives in Hawaii. I am aware of how disruptive religion has been on the world, but here it seemed to have a calming effect. In the local church, everyone knelt on the cement floor, completely topless. It was a peaceful, topless, Catholic Church.

By this time, we were entirely used to seeing both genders with bare breasts. This made me realize how much that is a bias from our European history. It was refreshing to see that on Satawal, Catholic influence and the native ways could merge so well.

I converted from shorts to one of those wraps the men wore; and it was more comfortable. 99 percent of everything consumed on the island came from Satawal or nearby islands. The cheap flip-flop shoes and noodles were the only manufactured products that were for sale. Breadfruit, taro, coconut, turtle or fish was what people ate, along with the occasional pig. Lard was the preferred grease to cook with.

All the festivities leading up to the ordination of the priest were taking place both inside the church and outside. There were probably a thousand people on this small island, all working in harmony. The  youth seemed to do their part without ever having to be asked. There seemed be no discipline or tension between young and old, just honor.

On my way home again on the Micro Spirit, I realized what a special place this was. There are virtually no tourists there. The people I talked to from the outside were more worried than the locals about how this area could get screwed up. Maybe these islands could be managed like the Galapagos Islands, with guides to protect the natural environment. But then, I didn't think that the native people should be protected like an endangered species. Maybe things just have to change. With climate change, these little islands and all their inhabitants may be the first places to vanish, even without the invasion of other cultures.

The other day I was out on my motorcycle and I dropped in unannounced on Frank Culp, who lives nearby. I was surprised to meet up with the young girl Frank had sponsored years ago, Star, and her husband with their new baby. Star and her brother came over here to go to high school. Her dad is doing outrigger voyages. Mau was a direct relative of hers. I didn't ask if her dad now used a GPS to navigate.

THIRTY

FINDING MORE FAMILY IN EUROPE

"There are only 1000 people in the world and the rest are extras."

My family was not closely knit. Around 1870 my dad's family had moved from the area in Europe that was Prussia to Indiana, to California, and then I had moved to Washington State. Now my daughter is in Texas. Once I received an email from Simon Niemier of Cologne, or Köln, Germany. He said we must be related. I emailed back and we started a conversation. This was a class project of his to look up someone with the same last name and my name was the top of the Niemier list at the time. Simon was close to my son's age and he was born in the same part of former Prussia that is now Poland. When he was young, his family moved to Germany because, after the Iron Curtain came down, the job prospects were better in Germany. It was great to have the Internet bring my extended family closer together.

After a while, we realized that we could just talk on the phone and we started keeping in touch. Simon sent pictures of himself and his brother. There was a striking resemblance between Simon and my father when he was younger. Also Simon's brother and my son Tristan had a lot of similarities. When I decided Hannah and I needed some time together, we traveled there and visited. It was great seeing a country with someone who is, well, family. Simon's father and mother didn't speak English, but Simon's mother adored Hannah and held her hand as they walked down the street. I spoke some German, but Polish was completely different. We then went to see Simon's grandmother on his mother's side of the family in Poland. This was a very old country that still showed a lot of Soviet influence.

Grandma and I could communicate perfectly without saying anything.

Simon's brother and wife also traveled with us around Poland, much of it by small car. The Poles are very proud of the mountains there; they reminded me of the Cascade Mountains near Bellingham. We toured the sad Auschwitz concentration camp left over from World War II.

For me this was great to know I had family everywhere. With Facebook, I could look up my last name and I discovered many relatives who seemed to all be related to the original cousins who moved to Indiana. On my mom's side, I have met up with a few of the close relatives but that family was here in America for many generations because they came over much earlier.

Also on Facebook, I kept in touch with my classmates from Malibu. As adults, we could really appreciate our past. They posted family pictures of their childhood, which made me understand much more about what was going on when at the time I was only focused on trying to grow up.

I felt like my life was finally coming together. I was finally a complete person. I wasn't dependent on any other family to make me happy. I could pick and choose whomever I wanted to be with, and I did. I didn't feel lonely.

Someone said you don't just have friendships, you have to make them. I consider my friends my biggest assets; they are worth more than anything I could ever own.

Reflections

This episode in my life was a major readjustment of all four of my Lover, Warrior, King, and Magician energies; or as I called them Dreamer, Hunter, Visionary, and Craftsman. My work-family, as well as my immediate family, had gone away. I was left pretty much alone, but independent. And for once in my life I had a supply of money, so I wasn't sweating that.

This new independence was hard to get used to. I didn't have anything to do or to visualize. Another gentleman, Bill Masters, sold his company at about the same time and was not included with new plans for the company after the sale. Bill and I were hopelessly ADD, and he was as lost as I was. He had no idea what to do with his energies either, so we switched from being fierce competitors to friends with the same problem: what to do now.

Being in the Moment

The hunter lives to solve problems and deal with the unexpected. In business, it is frequent that problem solving is needed. This is sometimes referred to as putting out fires; it happens when things either aren't thought out perfectly or are not executed according to plan. ADD hunters are addicted to this in-the-moment time like a drug.

Like it or not, after I sold my company, I found myself in an entirely different landscape. I lost all the support I had on the way up: my wife, my in-laws, my business colleagues, and my staff at work. I had achieved a huge and enviable success by selling the company, but I was in emotional free fall. Growing up, I spent a lot of time with other families. Then I moved into Rebecca's family, and even worked side by side with them. After the sale of Ocean Kayak and the divorce, I was without a tribe.

Who was I? For the first time in my life, I had to become completely my own person.

THIRTY-ONE

HOW DOES ATTENTION DEFICIT DISORDER FIGURE INTO ALL OF THIS?

"Or when policy fails just fake it."

I believe this subject deserves a whole chapter because it doesn't do it justice to fit it in and around everything else when ADD is such a big part of my life and maybe yours, too. For simplicity's sake, I will refer to ADD and ADHD only as ADD.

The Hunter

Many top entrepreneurs come equipped with ADD. I say equipped because I truly believe it is an asset in many cases. One author who made a lot of sense to me was Thomas Hartman, who compared people with ADD to hunters, and the rest as farmers. I reasoned that we are living in an ever-increasing agrarian or farmer-type society in more ways than just food. Hunters need a lot of room, and they function better when there are wilder things to be tracked down. "Hunting" can be anything from racing motorcycles to being an entrepreneur. The common thread is that hunter types are not afraid and may prefer to take risks and "make it big," instead of playing it safe for less reward. As we live in more and more populated cities, we have to act like "farmers" where there are a lot of repetitive tasks to do in smaller spaces that we have to fit tightly into.

In general, the main trait attributed to ADD is the inability to focus, or the tendency to get distracted easily. People with ADD are often accused of being unproductive, because they don't do things in the orderly manner that today's world expects. They tend to fidget and are always moving around. They often fit well into an athletic lifestyle. Then they can become hyper-focused on something and will not let it go until they master it. This reminds me of my cat, a supreme hunter. She sits around, seemingly unproductive, until she sees something out of the corner of her eye that no one else notices. Then she snaps into action and relentlessly hunts down the prize.

Often the ADD person has to feel or associate with objects in a three-dimensional way to feel comfortable with an understanding of them. Maybe this comes from the same thought process hunters have when they realize their approach must be perfect or they risk injury or death. The skeletons of early Neanderthals reveal many bones broken. Oddly enough, the number and position of breaks almost exactly parallel those of rodeo riders. If a Neanderthal were walking down the street, he would look pretty human but his bones would be much more robust.

214

One thing scientists know for sure is that Neanderthals had to walk to keep up with migrating game. If a Neanderthal broke an arm, the group would care for him and he would usually get back into action, but if his leg were broken, he would be left behind to die.

Running, or regular exercise, for the ADD hunter can be very beneficial to the way this type of person operates. This activity brings one into the "now zone," especially if the activity is something like surfing or mountain biking. These activities are typically not part of life growing up, so they must be learned. When I trained for the Ironman Triathlon, at first my mind thought it was really crazy to put my body through such apparent extremes. To my surprise, the resistance was all in my head. When my mind got used to the routine of training 10 to 16 hours a week, I had no problems. After that experience, I realized that movement was the natural or normal state for my body, because everything felt so great.

I don't know if this has anything to do with ADD, but since I am into the water I find it very interesting. The theory is that we, as a species, spent a considerable amount of time in the water. The reasoning goes like this: we are essentially hairless and all of the other hairless animals like the elephants, dolphins, whales, and even rhinos have spent time in the water as a species. A few aquatic animals have kept their hair, like seals. None of the other great apes have spent time in the water. The only animals that can hold their breath well have gone through this aquatic phase. What is also associated with holding one's breath is speaking.

215

None of the other apes can speak like we can. Dolphins and whales speak. Even the ability to walk on two feet could have come from being half submerged in water. Many of the other apes walk on two feet if they are in waist-deep water. Bonobo apes are genetically our closest relatives. They can walk upright but not to the extent we do, and they are not hairless.

Thom Hartmann says there is a specific gene that seems to be associated with novelty and ADD. He makes a good case for how it came about 40,000 years ago. Before that, we as humans had gone through a lot of adapting because of extreme climate changes that would happen every so often after people settled into villages and got comfortable. When the climate shifted, the people that left and were able to adapt to new environments survived. This seems to be a trait of ADD people. We are the first to get up and go.

After the climate settled down, the novel ideas started showing up in our development of civilization. The theory is that the people who got up and went were also responsible for many of the novel ideas that showed up later. Thom calls this the "Edison Gene" named for Thomas Edison, the inventor of the light bulb, and The Edison Gene is what Thom Hartmann named his book on the subject. The other book on ADD that I really like is Attention Deficit Disorder: A Different Perception, which has a lot of the hunter-farmer analogies. Thomas Edison would be the type of person who survived way back in more primitive times. My observation of people that seem to fit into the ADD category is that they seem to come alive when objects zip past them, rather than when they sit looking at those same objects. ADD types would rather race down a road lined with trees than sit back and gaze at those same trees. They would rather be "in" something rather than observe something. People with ADD often require more of a thrill than most "normal" people. The connections in the ADD brain have been compared to a spark plug with the gap set wide, requiring a greater thrill to make the spark plug work.

How My ADD Helped in the Workplace: Being Present with Passion

I read more about adult ADD, and found I perfectly matched the description. To summarize, I tried the meds and found certain things I did, like typing, would improve. At the time, I was carving out more and more complex shapes and I worried that any medication would make me less creative. Right after I took it, I had to carve out the Malibu. I noticed a slightly different feel to things but not nearly as intense as what I feel from a strong cup of coffee or even one beer. The Malibu became one of the most popular designs of all my kayaks and is still a leader because it does so many different things.

Creativity may actually improve with medication. We already self-medicate a lot with caffeine and alcohol. Both of these drugs are socially acceptable while pills carry the stigma that they are for crazy people. In my opinion, being a little crazy is not a bad thing. Remember, I was the one who considered the world becoming way too "normal," and being too "normal" can be worse than being a little crazy.

Being on meds made me feel sort of weird. I think this is because crazy people use "meds." Sane people use drugs like alcohol and tobacco. Right? On a one to ten scale where 10 has the strongest effect and zero is not perceptible, to me beer is a 7. Coffee is a 4 and ADD meds are about a 2. They are very effective in an efficient way, doing what they were designed for, at least for me.

The other profound difference I noticed when I was on the meds was that I could be fearless in business meetings. I was also taking Prozac, which is a very pure drug with very few side effects. ADD in the workplace is a recognized disability where the employee has every right to ask for a workspace that is free of distractions. It can also be up to the employee to look for jobs that fit her strengths and weaknesses, including tasks that may lend themselves to ADD strengths, rather than creating an unproductive struggle. Struggle is not always bad. The analogy of the free spirit being like the kite and the other person being like the string can lead to tough but very productive environments that can generate extraordinary results.

ADD Helps Me Solve Problems and Design

When I think about my desire to paddle out through the surf to get a thrill or my desire to go fast on a motorcycle, I believe those urges are directly related to my ADD. When I throw myself into a situation like the surf, I just have to react. I feel at home in that environment. When I consider an issue, I often think of it from being inside the problem rather than looking in at it. Being in a kayak in swells and constant movement in the ocean is to me like being a part of the ocean. One time I called kayaks "prosthetic devices for the aquatically challenged humans." Another activity that I like doing and may have something to do with this whole behavior is to get into a complex problem like a Sudoku puzzle and figure it out. I don't solve puzzles in an entirely logical way. I seem to be able to feel my way around the problem and then the answer just presents itself to me. When I carve little kayak models, often I only have a vague idea of what I want and then I let my hands carve it without letting my mind get in the way.

Using Rituals to Avoid Distraction

While growing up I had many teachers and other people try to tell me how bad I was at doing things. Now I realize it is either one of those lies that I believed or I just process information differently. I have relied on habit or ritual to keep from getting off track. I set the ritual with an intention and do it for long enough to become habit. It doesn't always work perfectly but struggle is also okay.

Struggle Creates Passion

Struggling with ADD can create passion, which can in turn can be much more appealing than an analytical process. The more I explain to others how ADD works for me, the better I understand it myself.

Reflections

Can you see how struggle can make for passion that can lead to great things for you? Do you understand the difference between struggle and repeated failure? Can you see the line where struggle becomes failure and doesn't lead to success? If you are struggling, can you see how ritual can create habits to avoid unwanted distracting behavior? Can you see how using rituals can be fun and a positive experience for you and others and doesn't have to be a dramatic experience?Do you see how choosing the right environment is your own responsibility?

THIRTY-TWO

IRONMAN AND PERSONAL DEVELOPMENT

"One mans confidence is a majority."

Jim Kreoufski, one of the main Banzai Bozos, had been a waterman for some time. He grew up in Oregon in a fishing community on the Oregon

221

Coast. He had joined the Coast Guard and spent a lot of time on the water in various parts of the world. He worked on a rescue team on the local level and other lifesaving organizations on the national level.

Jim lived in Hawaii on the big island for many years. Jim and Marsha lived on sailboats and had many adventures. Marsha was on an all-women's outrigger canoe team that went undefeated in races for a whole year. They both loved the islands and dreamed of returning after living in Northern California, where I met them. When Jim got a job offer from a construction firm to manage the high-end home construction in Kona on the big island, he took it and they moved there. Hawaii was also the home of the Ironman Triathlons. When I was visiting, Jim and I volunteered to hand out water to the athletes for the half Iron. The competitors looked like they were having so much fun that we looked at each other and said, "Let's do this next year."

We did the Half Iron together the next year and had a great time. The day afterwards, we had to climb the stairs slowly. The Half Iron wasn't really that hard physically, but it was easy to get jangled mentally. The swim was a little over one mile; the biking portion was 60 miles, up the main highway, followed by a 12-mile run. I was a slow runner with the same style as a gorilla but it didn't matter, because everyone was pretty slow at that point.

Just Keep the Legs Moving

John Culver, was a professional bicyclist in his youth and later a mountain climber who did guide work and fitness programs for climbers before they got to the mountain. His workouts were mainly outside, and wrote a book about that: Fit by Nature. His company, AdventX, trains people for climbs, then John leads the climbs in exotic places like Mount Kilimanjaro in Africa. John had done the full Ironman race once and convinced me that I could do it. All he said was "Keep your legs moving," and I believed him.

Once I got over the false belief that I couldn't do it, it was just a matter of putting in the time to train and then running the race. John had a wonderful way of enabling me to believe I could do it. The training can be broken down into weekly segments that build in intensity, followed by a week of lighter workouts, then  another intense build until the peak just before the event. Training really turned out to be just putting in the hours around the weather and my time with the kids. The schedule was usually a hard day, then a recovery day with one long and hard day per week.

Many of my workouts could be done indoors on a bike trainer. Heart rate is key, because if you keep that under a certain level, you can go all day but if your heart rate is too high for more than an hour and a half, your muscles break down and you "bonk" (run out of steam). The other issue is nutrition, because after a few hours you need to eat and drink to replace calories lost. It took me about 14 hours to do the first Ironman and food was important. I eventually got a training schedule from a guy in New Zealand whom I never met. The schedule was on a computer printout and I tend to follow information presented that way. I learned that I could get to higher performance levels when I rigorously followed a schedule.

I did three Ironman races in Penticton, Canada, and two more in Coeur d'Alene, Idaho. All of them were a lot of fun. By now, I found that my body would do most anything I asked of it. My barriers had been mostly mental. The triathlon community was very strong and they were great people to be around. The training forced me to be outside, which I enjoyed, although in winter it can get cold if the bike breaks and you find yourself stranded. The great thing about these races is that everyone is a winner. You aren't racing for first place unless you are trying to qualify for the big race in Kona every year or be a professional triathlete. These people are the top five percent, the rest of us were just trying to finish. We celebrate finishing, or even starting.

The volunteers outnumber the athletes two to one, and there are typically 2,000 to 3,000 athletes in a race, all starting at once. The energy is thick. Then everyone starts the 2.4-mile swim and the competitors spread out pretty quickly. The racers spend the whole day in the present moment. Nothing else matters. The volunteers and spectators do a lot to keep you motivated, even miles away from the finish.

The 19-to 64-Year-Old Endurance Zone

I am fascinated with endurance because many people can succeed at building endurance. It doesn't require a special body type or build. The variety of body types out there on the racecourse is really amazing. People who are or were overweight might pass you right up. All the top finishers are as skinny as ET, however. Who cares? They are in a world of their own.

I read about a study about the best age for endurance sports, which include activities like mountain climbing. It turned out to be lower 30s. This seems to be true for the Tour de France bicycle racers. The starting age in the study was 19. Guess at what older age competitors got back to the same endurance performance as those who were 19? According to this book, it was 64! Now I am 64 and much of my performance, especially my endurance, is the same as when I was 19. Even most weightlifting is the same.

I Take Up Flying

I still have my father's pilot's logbook from 1936 when he took lessons. He wanted to fly for the RAF in World War II. He ended up in the U.S. Army, and didn't have the college credits to become a pilot so he was a crew chief,  or lead mechanic, in the South Pacific during the war. My brother was a helicopter pilot in Viet Nam and in Germany. I figured it was my turn to carry on the family tradition. My dream was to fly to the west coast of Vancouver Island in a floatplane. Like triathlon training, pilot training is pretty structured. The flight school had computer courses for the textbook parts of the course. I got frustrated about having to do each lesson several times before I got the test correct. I also worried that my ADD would make me get distracted so I would forget something. Then I then realized there was no one sitting beside me competing with me, as there had been in school. It didn't matter if I needed to read the chapter five times. A year from now, that still wouldn't matter.

The time I spent in the air was beautiful and I especially enjoyed the float training because there were no airports to contend with. I learned that one of the most dangerous things for a floatplane is mirror-smooth water because that surface makes it hard to know exactly when the plane will touch down. If there is a little ripple on the surface it is easier to judge distance. However, if the surface chop is over one foot, that's too dangerous to land in. Fog and weather on the coast are big factors. It is said that the clouds have rocks in them on the coast, and you'd better believe it.

Weather reports in remote regions aren't very reliable so you have to adapt to changing conditions. One time when I flew to Nuchatlitz, I thought I would have to land elsewhere because the whole area looked fogged in. But just for the heck of it I flew to where my GPS said Nuchatlitz was, and presto, there was a tiny quarter-mile long hole in the fog below. I quickly descended through it and landed. For the next few days I stayed there and built a large table. Everything in the outside world could wait, and it did. The special moments in the air are memories that will never leave my mind. In the whole of my life, these special memories are what I seek.

Mankind Project and New Warrior Training

After all the triathlon racing, John Culver told me about a group called Mankind Project. There was a weekend called New Warrior Training. It didn't sound like any weapons were involved, so I decided to go for it sight unseen. During the New Warrior Training weekend, the team uses techniques that force you to find your own resistance or fears by going back to their source in your past. This is not the shrink type of talking about your childhood from a distance on a couch sort of thing. They got me, and every man present, to relive our past with all the emotions that went with it.

After the weekend, there was a local group I could attend that didn't cost anything but took donations. There the real work of dismantling a lifetime of unnecessary and untrue belief systems can happen. This process is virtually impossible to do on your own. A group as witness is essential. I had a lot of conversations and even wrote letters to my dead father to straighten out our relationship in my head. These conversations would have been good to have when he was alive.

227

An associated program, called Boys to Men, is an initiation to being a man for boys under 18. Much of the work suggests that modern man leaves home and goes away to work and isn't present to teach his son how to be a man or his daughter how to relate to men. The result is that many men nowadays are just grown-up boys. A lot of the theories are based on Carl Jung and the archetypes Lover, Warrior, Magician, King, so it is not new stuff.

The Boys to Men weekend was almost totally run by journeymen who were still under 18 but had been through this program before. I carpooled with two brothers who said this was the best weekend of their entire lives. This weekend created deep bonds between my son Tristan and me. We may disagree or even fight at times, but deep down we are connected. I don't mind being vulnerable around him. I can always say I love him, and he says the same. We trust and respect each other.

Some excellent books that made me rethink relationships were, Getting the Love You Want, by Harville Hendrix, and The Way of the Superior Man, by David Deida. Getting the Love You Want describes attraction and love as identifying your lover as someone like one of your caregivers when you were small. That person feels so familiar you fall in love with them, which is partially caused by a chemical in our heads. But then, after the love chemistry wears off, that person brings back all the painful parts of growing up which are really our hot buttons. If this situation is recognized and handled in a mature way, the person whose buttons are pushed is able to get close to those fears and deal with them and can thank the button pusher, because he or she is the only person close enough to push those buttons in the first place.

The second book, The Way of the Superior Man, was given to me by my lifelong friend, Nancy Bennetts. I find it interesting that some women are offended by the title while others are delighted by it. The book describes what a modern relationship could be like. The author describes the 1950s relationships as being unrealistically typecast, where women didn't work and only raised kids and men did nothing but work. Decades later, feminists said they wanted equality but confused this with recognizing no difference between men and women with no tension and placid relationships. David Deida explains that the two are equal but different.

THIRTY-THREE

MEETING TRACY ON THE ALASKA FERRY

"Something to do, someone to love, something to hope for."

Nancy Bennetts told me she was leaving on the ferry to Alaska in July to take a trip with her daughter Allison. My brother and I had two BMW motorcycles that were perfect for such a trip. Up to this time, we seemed to be able to stand each other only for about three days and now we were planning a three-week trip.

231

Nancy had reserved a stateroom, which we thought would be handy. On that Friday afternoon I drove five miles down to the ferry terminal, we loaded, met up with Nancy and  Allison, and we were off. My brother Jul and I set up our tents on the deck, which turned out to be a much better sleeping arrangement than the stateroom. The Alaska Ferry is sort of a blue-collar affair with only a few staterooms. Almost everyone sleeps in tents on deck or inside on recliner-type chairs. The ferry stops at various places along the marine highway in little towns like Ketchikan. I talked to a biker who said there are only 42 miles of road in Ketchikan and 42 motorcycles, mostly Harleys. While there, we visited a neighbor, Vince, who was working on a John Sayles movie, Limbo, which is a great story and accurately describes life in small town costal Alaska.

Alaska is still a wild place where bears can run right through town and moose bigger than horses can run right out on any road. Luckily, we only saw one dead moose but they were always on our mind.

When in Anchorage my brother's Beemer started to make a funny noise. We thought it was the driveshaft, so he filled the usually dry space with oil and the noise went away. We thought that fix would work until we made it home. One of the consequences of having that problem was that we decided to take the ferry down to the paved road part of Canada and not go on the gravel Alcan Highway, which I didn't care to do anyway because it would be full of campers that would go slow and create lots of dust, making it hard and dangerous to pass. After a few weeks of adventure in Alaska, we loaded the bikes on the ferry south.

Meeting Tracy

The Alaska Ferry, or any of the ferries in the northwest, is good place to meet all sorts of people. I met Tracy, a Canadian, who had hiked the Chilkoot Trail, the famous  historical route that all the gold diggers traveled 100 years earlier in 1897. We both liked backpacking and loved the outdoors. We talked and were clearly attracted to each other, but were both in other relationships at the time. We kept in touch and, years later, got together. For a long time, we would just meet one day a week for a mid-week vacation. Tracy told her friends about me and would refer to me as her "Wednesday guy." Sometimes she would venture down to Bellingham. She drove an old Ford van that she used for the vending machine business that she owned and ran. Tracy got the business from her dad, and that was another thing we shared: a love for business.

We got engaged, went through all the immigration stuff, and after a lot of waiting, we had a wedding at the courthouse. Our honeymoon was a little rough, because we took her two girls and my son and daughter to a triathlon in Oregon. But somehow we survived.

Even though Tracy grew up only an hour north of Bellingham, it was Canada, and it took her quite a while to adjust to this new land with different people. As Americans we often overlook the differences in other cultures. The Canadians have a lot of pride in being Canadians. The population of Canada is only one tenth the size of the U.S. population and the country gets overshadowed and discounted easily. I think Canadians are different at the core and are more community or family minded, while Americans stress independence. A few years ago the most popular type of car in the U.S. was the SUV, while in Canada it was the minivan. Also a few years back, Canada wanted to identify its greatest hero. One would think it would have to be Wayne Gretzky the hockey legend or Terry Fox who after losing a leg to cancer decided to run across the whole of Canada. It was neither. It was Tommy Douglas, who created the Canadian universal health care system decades ago. The two areas in which Canadians pride themselves on superior to the U.S. are hockey and health care.

Tracy got the triathlon bug when she saw me complete the Ironman in Canada. Tracy signed up for the next year's Ironman. The only problem was that Tracy couldn't swim, which didn't deter her one bit because she had a whole year to learn. Months later, she reported that she did half of the Ironman swim distance of 1.2 miles in half the maximum time before the cutoff. Running was pretty easy for Tracy and working up to marathon distance wasn't as hard for her as the swim. The biking was a matter of putting in the training hours. Even if we didn't always train together, having the same interest was fun.

After hundreds of hours of training, race day came. Tracy made the swim under the maximum time and was off on the bike. On the bike, she got a flat but got it fixed. However, in a few miles it went flat again. This time the guys that drive the truck helped her fix it. It went flat again. There was a small hole in the tire, which takes a few miles to go flat again. Eventually she sat down and cried because she realized she wouldn't make the bike time cutoff.

Tracy can be very determined so the next year I made sure the tires were good and assembled a good repair kit with two extra tubes. We both raced and she finished. We loved these events because there were no losers. I think every participant is a winner the minute they show up and start.

Reflections

The mind and body are connected. One doesn't work without the other. I believe Aristotle said, "Sound body and sound mind."

Jim Lohr in his writing says that energy management is more important than time management, and that means you shouldn't do anything for more than three hours at a stretch. Studies show that sitting for more than an hour is really bad for your health and   vigorous exercise several times a day can be beneficial to productivity.

For those with ADD, it is healthy to vary the activities. Physical activity while doing a job enables us to focus on what we are doing. When I design kayaks, I hand carve them with sanders in a small one-sixth scale. I can feel the curve of the lines far better than I can see them.

The Importance of Ritual

It can be hard to find the time to work out, and if you're like me, you put it off till the end of the day and then you rush through it, so your workout is not really as thorough as it should be. I heard of Nelson Mandela running right in his jail cell where he was for decades. He kept in good shape and it kept him mentally strong. One day I was watching my coffee drip through the coffeemaker, and I thought that I could be running right then. I did jumping jacks instead.

You Can Reinvent Yourself

A workout can be a good time to think about your life from a higher place. Where is your life now and where it is going? Are you achieving your goals? Are your goals relevant? Do your goals mean anything to you or are you chasing the goals for your parents or spouse?

Is fear holding you back? Do you like the challenges you have before you? Could you use a structured challenge like training for the Ironman triathlon? Be open to finding a new group of friends, tackling new challenges, and celebrating a whole new life.

THIRTY-FOUR

SHOULD I REALLY DO THIS BUSINESS THING AGAIN?

"Nostalgia isn't what it used to be."

Although I enjoyed my time away from managing Ocean Kayak, I really missed all the interaction of being in a business. I thought it would be easy to just set up another rotomolding company and make some kayaks and watercraft on the side for fun. I could get a core group of people together and the company would practically run itself. There was a building available just south of Bellingham, and I signed a lease for more space than I needed and created my new company, Wild Design, Inc. The rent was cheap for the time, but the money still amounted to a lot per month. I learned that the market had changed and rotomolding had become a lot more competitive over the decade I was not working in that field. We built our own molding machine, which was a disaster and had a very slow cycle time, which limited its profitability. Sales of custom molding or doing molding for other companies, was also difficult, and much harder than selling our own products.

NuCanoe

One of the water products that did come out of Wild Design was the NuCanoe, which was essentially a sit-on-top canoe. The foot area was below the waterline and the sides of the boat were not too high, but  the idea was that if the boat flipped there was enough flotation that you could paddle to shore or bail it out easily. We took pictures of me sitting on the side of the boat with my feet in the water.

We had problems with the details. When the boat cooled, it would shrink, and if not handled properly it would lose flotation. Air had to be pumped into the boat as it was cooling, to end up with more flotation. Also, our cycle time was so slow that we could not possibly make enough of products and money to pay our expenses.

Later I sold the molds to Blake Young who honed in on that business and nursed it along with TLC until it was popular. He has since come out with many more models after he made the first one profitable through a lot of hard work and attention to getting the details right.

Making False Assumptions

It is easy to assume that if a plan worked once, it would work again. A company is like an orchestra that has been honing its sound over decades. It is too easy to come from that sort of environment and assume that the next one will just happen that way, too.

With Ocean Kayak I had built great business relationships years before I went into full-on production. Also, I was very lucky being at the right place at the right time to crank up production and sales of sit-on-top kayaks just after the Windsurfer industry collapsed.

When things aren't going well business-wise, there is a tendency to put every last dollar into the enterprise to see if you can "turn it around," which is what I did. In retrospect, I should have cut my losses much sooner. I should have waited until I had the promise of profitable business before spending money on a lot of equipment and especially on a five-year lease.

Once you have money, investing it can seem pretty dull, but putting your riches into real estate or income property can be wise even though it is not very exciting or interactive. If one is making enough money in investments, then your new business can be smaller and more of a hobby. It can even lose money if your investments make up for that loss.

After Wild Design collapsed and I had spent a lot of money chasing it, I had to find something to do with myself. I thought I could create a virtual company with no employees. I had heard about Marin Bicycles in California who just got all of their bikes made offshore and only had about five people in the office managing shipments and sales. Maybe this could work for me.

In Timothy Ferriss' book, The 4-Hour Workweek, he describes getting all sorts of work done through the Internet using foreign companies whose employees worked for much less than employees in America. One person could set up production somewhere or just buy something and sell it with minimal management. This would allow you to travel all over the place. One thing he said that was interesting was to get rid of all your possessions so you could be unencumbered. I was still getting comfortable with my nest of stuff that didn't really cost me much.

Struggling with Computers and Communication

I found it was really difficult to do the simplest things that Ferris described doing on the computer. I thought I would learn somehow. What I didn't realize was that the technology was not static, so I was always catching up. I was an Internet immigrant and one of the last to get on the boat. I tried putting together websites, but hated maintaining them. All I wanted to do was create new stuff. I did stick with it, but could never manage to use things like Facebook as a sales tool

.

Getting into Consulting: It's Okay Not to Own the Company

I found that I could help
other companies grow,
which was really like a
mentoring process. It was
very satisfying watching the
parts of these companies
come together without
having to be "in charge." My ego had to jump in the back seat
sometimes, but it was an interesting view from there. As much as I
didn't like managing my own projects, I enjoyed managing other
people's projects.

I would start by offering 10 hours and usually charging under $2000 to
tell them how much their boat would weigh and cost to make and then I
usually made a scale model. I found that after an hour or so of casual
conversation, I would find out if they were serious. Anybody that
couldn't afford $2000 probably wasn't going very far anyway, and
should just keep talking about it only to someone other than me. I really
believed that my experience could save them a lot of time and money. I
told every potential client that if they wanted to take four decades and
gather the experience that I had, they could save a few bucks. The other
argument I made was that by hiring me, their learning curve could be
minimized, and then they could make more money earlier.

After the person wanting to start the company held my scale model, the product became real for them, and they were ready to start. From there, we could make a CAD model from which we would determine all the waterlines and do other calculations. We never did speed or stability calculations, because I didn't trust the accuracy. We would then cut a full-sized model with my CNC machine, usually out of Styrofoam. This foam model prototype would get fiber glassed and then it could be field tested and even market tested.

Consulting on the Diablo Fishing Kayak

One of the first consulting jobs I did was with a couple of guys from Austin, Texas, which is a town a lot like Bellingham in that it is small and liberal and full of creative people. The company was Diablo

Paddlesports. We started in the spring and the goal was to be able to sell product that same year. Usually a company starting something in the spring banks on the next year. If you sell to dealers, they do all their buying in the fall of the previous year for the next spring.

The Diablo boats were designed and made in only two months, which enabled them to sell an extra season and put them a year ahead. The guys behind this project were young, which is what the industry needed because many of the kayak community were Baby Boomers who were not getting any younger. It was refreshing to see the young energy at work. The Diablo itself was similar to a big surfboard, not unlike my very first sit-on-top kayak except it was three feet wide and would hold probably three times the weight. The total weight of the craft was probably under 60 pounds and probably about 20 pounds less than an equivalent rotomolded kayak. This craft could also be paddled standing up, like a paddleboard. You can see the fish much further off when standing than when sitting down, and also you can see the fish next to the boat and the bottom much more easily.

This was the first boat that I designed to be vacuum formed. Vacuum forming requires cheap molds but expensive sheets. You can get into business making expensive boats or kayaks, which look really good and are light and shiny, with not much money to get started. The sheet material has a glossy layer and lasts longer than fiberglass. These kayaks usually sell for between $1000 and $2000 from molds that only cost about $10,000. Rotomolded kayaks retail for $500 to $1,000 with molds that are $25,000 to $40,000.

Consulting for Kajun Custom Kayaks

The Kajun Custom Kayaks or KC Kayaks Company was run by three young guys who each had his specialty. This was a fun project because we designed the sides to come up higher and put in tracks for the seat to ride on. The seat could be flipped to make a high seat for standing easily in calm water or flipped down for more stability. At only 12.5 feet long, the boat would hold two large adults and still not take on water through the scuppers. The hull went from a single bow to a two-part hull with a tunnel in the rear. This made for a very stable configuration that was only 34 inches wide. The original boats were close to 50 pounds in weight, which made them easy to handle.

Gaines Garret was the overall manager, Corey did the production, and Andrew focused on sales. They found that to get a high quality product for their area, they had to make it themselves. They also made other models, including a Scout boat for the Boy Scouts. The Kajun Kayak is the closest to an original canoe but still a sit-on-top with all of the safety that comes with that design. These three guys make up a great team.

Consulting for Top Dog: The Paddleboard with a Chair

Top Dog was a group of three guys, each with various talents who had a great idea of making a fishing paddleboard with a chair on it. I had done a paddleboard made from thermo-formed, or vacuum-

formed, ABS sheet material, but had difficulty adhering the EPS Styrofoam to the skins. Tom Derrer at Eddyline Kayaks formed the two halves for me. Tom was also forming halves for Tahoe SUPs (Stand Up

Paddleboards) who were doing what I was trying to do. Sometimes different plastics and the glues involved don't work as well as you think they will. We did some tests with the hollow shape that came together in the middle. We used flexible resin to be like the vacuum-formed ABS so we could approximate the flex.

The unique part of this board was the seat and the track that the bottom of it fit into. I made a few prototype seats for them out of bent electrical conduit pipe and they actually worked pretty well and folded down nicely when not in use. The seat was a novel idea, and the company got a patent on it. This enabled a beginner to get in with confidence and not even have to stand up to paddle. An extra-long kayak paddle worked well for the seated position.

Weight was really important. The ABS would have to be pretty thin and after it got formed, it might get paper-thin. In vacuum forming, you have to pick out the thickness of the material to be formed and that is what you have to work with, unlike rotomolding where if you want the part to be thicker, you just add more material. I would recommend that the first run of material be thicker to be safe; then you can see where it could be thinner to save weight.

We formed the beautiful white-colored sheets, trimmed them out, and put the foam in just as planned. The process was critical because the two halves had to be stuck together before the seaming. The seaming was called a "shoebox seam" because the top went down over the bottom, which tucked inside. The internal parts had to be cut perfectly for the seam to work. Then the measurements had to be perfect to make the seam work well. Everything worked well, including the seaming. We used an adhesive that would harden in about ten minutes, which meant that by the time we made it all the way around the board the spot where we started was already hard.

The next day, we pulled the tape off the sides to hold the seam in place and the boards seemed nice and light. The Top Dog paddleboard paddled really well with one person or two, or one person and two dogs. I really liked the way the water exited cleanly off the stern with very little drag. We found that there was not really a good place to hold on to the board, so we retrofitted a handle.

Unfortunately, the ABS had been too thin and fractured in the places that stretched in the forming process. We tried a few things to fix the problem, but none of the solutions was satisfactory.

Everyone lost interest in the project before trying thicker ABS, which I felt would have solved the problem. The molds remained in my yard for the next few years, and then a friend of mine in San Diego said he ran into one of the team and they said they were coming out with a new paddleboard called the Cruiserboard. It was made in the U.S. out of a very strong material that you could hammer on without dinging the board. The company decided to make pretty much the same shape as before, which was really high volume so even out of the new material the weight is now 60 pounds. This isn't that heavy if you use wheels to get the paddleboard to the beach and don't lift it onto the car by yourself. It is a board for two, after all. To make it any lighter would make it very fragile. The seat is still there in the design and it's still a great concept for the casual user.

Tahoe SUP

Tahoe SUP perfected this process. They got the Styrofoam and ABS recipe to work with a few more adjustments for a product that could be made in the U.S., looks really great, and doesn't require all the labor that forces most SUPs to be manufactured offshore.

Just before the last Outdoor Retailer show, Tahoe SUP owner, Nathan, had all the parts to assemble a few for the show with next to no time to spare. It was Saturday night (yes, this is what boat builders and board Bozos do on some Saturday nights). The Tahoe team was going to pull an all-nighter when they discovered that the foam was slightly too large. James Thomas, who was directing things, looked up and saw another piece of foam just above the CNC machine and asked me if he could use it and I said, "No problem." Nathan went to sleep in his sprinter van in the driveway. The boards made it to the OR show and were a huge success. Where else in North America could one re-make a foam blank and have it ready by 8:00 am Sunday morning, a week before the show starts? The board was a big success at the show a week later and it had BIC Paddle Boards looking at it after hours trying to figure out how they made it. The price point for this board was under $1000 retail. At that price, this board could be a game changer.

THIRTY-FIVE

KIDS KAYAK AND THE LIFETIME COMPANY

"There is no future in Old Age"

In business, it can pay off to have lifelong friendships. Some people in the industry are close friends that you may never do business with; and after knowing others for years, you end up working together when the time is right. Malcolm Gladwell talks about this in his book, The Outliers.

In this case, my contact was Tom Eckert. Like me, he grew up in Southern California, although he grew up in the valley and drove out to the beaches. We were about the same age and he had done construction during one of the many building booms in Southern California and then had managed a rotomolding shop for a good friend of Elmer Good's.

Tom and I would share stories at rotomolding conferences about the various successes or complete failures in the industry and chuckle if it wasn't us we were talking about. We both knew and revered Elmer Good's presence in the industry and admired what he had done as an early pioneer and even what he may have failed to do over the years.

Over the course of a few decades, Tom had moved into working in sales for companies that did blow molding. With his background in production, Tom knew what was possible to build out of this medium and what would not work. He then paid for his own small kayak mold to be made and had a small inconspicuous booth at the large OR trade show that would mostly go unnoticed. Tom wanted to make a kid's kayak with goals of a retail price under $100 including a paddle, creating a kayak that would sell itself.

Along with the idea that this kid's kayak should be the ultimate impulse-buy, the other goal was to have the kayaks fit on a pallet that could be rolled right onto the showroom floor so the boat would sell with no help from the staff. When the supply ran out, the staff didn't even have to go back in the back and get another kayak. All they had to do is roll out another pallet. At six feet long, the kayaks were small enough to put right into a shopping cart. In Canada they were sold at a store called

MEC (Mountain Equipment Co-op), right at the cash register, so the customers could just pop one in the cart as they checked out.

Tom and I both had small planes and Tom had enough money, $40,000, to buy one mold. But production really required two, which meant he would have to sell the plane to buy the second mold, so instead he asked me if I could design the kayak and take a royalty for investing in the second mold.

This seemed simple enough. However, by this time I had realized that Tom had a way of never taking the time to really describe what was important and what was not important for the design. I asked at first what size box this kayak would have to fit into, so at least I knew the overall size. I calculated that with such a short kayak, to support a 130-pound kid would mean that we could only round off the corners of the block.

When I got into rotomolding kayaks, the process was considered too expensive and complicated for a small business to even attempt. There was only one other company, Perception, who was doing large-scale kayak production other than the first kayak that Elmer's Hollowform Company was making. When I made my own rotomolding machine, many other kayak companies must have thought, if that idiot Tim Niemier can do it, we can do it. After that many other kayak companies jumped into rotomolding. I even sold my first oven to Ann Dwire of Kiwi Kayak.

If Tom and I could pull this off, we could be in the blow molding business and manufacture products from our home office and home shop. Blow molding is much more efficient and much cheaper than rotomolding. Without any hardware, a blow-molded kayak only would cost us about a dollar a pound. The kid's kayak weighs less than 20 pounds, which is how it could sell for $100 retail in big box stores. In blow molding, polyethylene is extruded in a vertical cylinder, sandwiched between two molds that come together, and air is blown into the polyethylene cylinder, forcing the plastic to conform to the molds around it. After that shaping, the molds cool the thin plastic. This process has a very short cycle time of only a few minutes, unlike rotomolding, which takes over an hour.

The design and setup is very important. Once the mold is put onto the machine, it generally takes a run of 600 to 1000 kayaks to pay for the cost of setting up the production run in the first place. The bottom line is that the manufacturing cost and retail price of a kayak can be half to one third of the cost of the same kayak produced by rotomolding. Like early rotomolding, at the time Tom and I worked together, blow molding was too frightening for most kayak companies to even consider.

I was too big to test the kid's kayak. Testing such a shape was pretty easy for Tom because he said just make sure it works well. For me, that was much more difficult because I could not paddle the kayak myself and feel how it handled. I used to say that kayaks are like prosthetic devices for aquatically challenged humans. In other words the kayak is like a fake leg with a big shoe that you put on; the shape allows you to go through the water more efficiently than swimming. Kayaks are much faster and more comfortable.

I put an ad in the local university paper for a kayak tester who was no more than 110 pounds. I got tons of responses from guys who neglected to read the weight restrictions. Then, finally, wahoo! I got this wonderful petite college student, who was also in our local circus. Yes, Bellingham has its own local circus, so she was in good shape and was perfect for the job. Her long blond dreadlocks looked great in the pictures that I would use to show Tom what the boat looked like.

My talent was in being able to picture how the whole thing should generally look and then make a small model. James Thomas and I worked the model over but at one point or another it had been modeled in a CAD format that was not very precise and made uneven curves so none of the lines were constant or what I would consider good looking. The goal was a length of only six feet. It was difficult to make the kayak that short; the stern was wide and the seat had to be pretty far back to have any room for one's legs and feet. I added two little wedges to the back underside of the kayak to help propel it forward in a straight line, like the feathers on darts. The wedges worked pretty well. I couldn't paddle the kayak myself, so I had to sense how it felt by asking the college student and watching what happened when she stopped paddling. I wanted to get younger children to try it and once we had a young boy scheduled and then all of a sudden he froze and didn't want to sit in it. Maybe it was because too many people were watching. After a lot of remote testing on flat water I felt we had a winner.

I thought we really should try it in the surf. We loaded up everyone and drove four and a half hours south of Seattle and west of Olympia to the town of Westport, which is the most popular surf spot in Washington State. I had made a Styrofoam prototype and coated it with a sort of paint that wasn't as strong as fiberglass but I thought would work fine. That weekend there was huge surf, but I figured we would find a place somewhere to test it. The tide level formed a large inshore zone filled with safe smaller waves that re-formed from larger ones breaking way offshore. I wanted to get some video so I had to be able to be in the water standing no more than up to my waist. My college student paddled out and caught a few waves, but usually the boat turned sideways and she fell over, getting sand into her long dreadlocks. The waves were coming in surges that lasted about 30 seconds. It wasn't really dangerous and she was a good swimmer. We got some great shots and right at the end the small kayak prototype broke into two pieces when a wave smacked it!

The first sales of the kid's kayak were really good. Tom was meticulous about every detail. The mold worked well and the first sales were really good.

By now the kayak market was getting pretty diverse and a lot of the "serious" kayakers and kayak companies were unaware that this kid's kayak even existed. They were amazed when I told them that there was a $99 kayak on the market. This wasn't something they had even considered. The kids' kayaks were also an item that took up only a few square feet of floor space in stores where they calculated how much money it made per square foot. Kayaks have always been really bad at returning much money per square foot of display space; they usually take too long to sell and take up too much space. This kid's kayak fit nicely into the retail world and was profitable. Recently I lost a little weight and could just balance on the kids' kayak and found it paddled well and was extremely portable.

THIRTY-SIX

THE WAVE

"Sell to the classes live with the masses,
sell to the masses live with the classes."

Sales of the kid's kayak, now called the "Wave," went through the roof because it was such a casual purchase. I was thrilled to get the royalty checks, which were quite good. I didn't have to do anything or manage anything after I shipped out the pattern to make the mold from. The company that made these kayaks for North America was Lifetime, who got their start making the portable basketball backboards that are in many people's driveways and are filled with water to hold them down. The company grew quickly and was always looking for more items to run through their machines. They could make tons of products pretty quickly and it was better to have the machines making something than sitting idle. Tom used them for some of the other kayaks that he designed.

Pretty soon, Lifetime decided they should get into this business themselves, so they bought Tom's company, Dragonfly Innovation.

At that time, Lifetime sold about 500 million worth of products per year, and the kayaks could add another 100 million in a few years. When Lifetime bought Dragonfly Innovation, they didn't want me to get a royalty like before, so we agreed to a cash-out. There was also an agreement for future design work, but the end date for that didn't extend very far into the future. Lifetime wanted to get into the paddlesports business, but wanted to do it right.

While at Ocean Kayak, I had thought of creating a kid's kayak, but never found the time. The only sit-on-top kayak I created that came close was the Yakboard, which was eight feet long and would take a medium-sized adult like me. When John Mann paddled one of the black prototypes of this model out around Seattle, a pod of orcas passed by and a baby orca swam right over to have a closer look at this baby black kayak. I had no problem building mass-market kayaks if that got more butts in boats.

Building a Folding Kayak

A folding kayak would be as easy to sell as the kids kayak. Tom really believed that if the kid's kayak sold because it was easy to just pick up and take home, a folding kayak would be also easy  to sell. I worked very hard to make the folding kayak. I designed it to Tom's specifications, because I felt that combining different solutions to the tricky problem of the locking mechanism would confuse things. I did try to make one with one-inch webbing and a cam buckle that tightened down the webbing. I made it so that the webbing would be locked from the top but would serve to lock the bottom together. Locking the kayak open from top was more convenient and took only seconds to set up.

 Tom was worried that the webbing would stretch when it got wet and would not hold the parts rigid and then the kayak would start to fold in the water. The hinges had to be on the top because the upward curve of the bow had to fold into the seat area. The bottom formed the flatter outside surfaces of the package. All together it made a fairly small box-like structure that could go into the back seat

of most cars. The other big advantage was that it could not only fit on a pallet but also go on shelves in retail stores. This could change paddlesports because not only could people get the kayak to the car but also they didn't have to put the kayak on top of the car. If a mom and kids wanted to get this kayak for Father's Day, they could put it in the back of their hatchback, which made it an impulse buy for anybody.

Making the folding kayak prototype was a royal pain, and a week before the show Tom wanted me to completely redo it using a different material. I worked for 20 hours a day to get it done and finished everything except for painting it. Tristan came down with me and helped drive the 15 hours to Salt Lake City. Driving was the only way we could get the prototype there in time and I was in no shape to drive that far without falling asleep. When we finally got to Lifetime, the R&D guy, Mike, spent all night painting the prototype so it was ready the next day when the show started. We made it happen.

An even more amazing thing happened just as I was about to get frustrated with all the last minute work I had taken on to complete this folding kayak prototype for the show. I was in extreme sleep deficit and operating on automatic pilot. People somehow got my name as the person to talk to about the kid's kayak. I love the feedback although it was usually a request for a drain plug that fell out. There was an email from a lady who said her daughter had some sort of attention deficit that was way more extreme than ADD or ADHD. Her daughter could not hold anything together to focus. It sounded like her attention was just all over the place. Worse yet, she seemed to realize she had a problem when she saw her sister, who didn't have the distraction disability, paddle around effortlessly.

The mother emailed me to say that the daughter who was completely distracted could focus when she was paddling in the kid's kayak! For me, it was a very powerful emotional charge because the kayaks had given me the same focus. My life would be so scattered without this intense love for being on the water. The water had been the same saving grace for me as it had been for the little girl. I cried right then and there. I wrote the little girl's mother back and said to somehow someday thank her daughter, because this experience made me aware of my life's work. The mom even sent me a video of her daughter paddling. I felt so blessed that I was able to affect this little girl and her mother in such a profound way. The most amazing things can happen at the most unlikely times.

People loved the kid's kayak and the other line of kayaks, but didn't understand the folding kayak. Lifetime thought of it like a folding bicycle and thought the market was limited so didn't pursue it for a number of months but did register for a patent on the mechanism. After a year the patent has to be formally applied for, or it is lost. I told Lifetime that even though this was officially part of Tom's Dragonfly Innovation, I had not been compensated for the work I did on it, so it seemed logical to either give me that model and the rights to make it or pay me. Lifetime gave me the whole thing, so I went ahead with the formal patent application with my local patent attorney, Mike Schacht

THIRTY-SEVEN

THE ORIGAMI PADDLER PADDLEBOARD IS BORN

"The best way to have one good idea is to start with 100 first"

Could I create a crowd funded, one-person business with no employees? The key to creating my new product was the folding feature, because that meant that I didn't need the huge infrastructure of dealers or have to hassle with the trucking companies to ship this product. I could ship them to anywhere from anywhere, even from my house. I figured that if I could make my new product fold and be shippable by UPS, it should be easy to sell with the work subcontracted out.

I had never crowd funded a business but I thought it would be worth a try. If Amazon bought and sold it, that could take care of direct sales. My goal was to sell something for about $1000 retail. If I could do all the marketing myself, I would only have to sell 200 of them to make $100,000. I knew I might need some help setting up the crowd funding.

I wanted to make a folding paddleboard, not a kayak. After rethinking the whole concept of a folding kayak, I thought it would be better as a folding paddleboard because that segment of the paddlesports market was growing much faster than kayaks, which were a larger segment but had pretty flat growth. I figured out a way to limit the length of the webbing so if it couldn't stretch by much. Also, I made the board fold completely into thirds, so that each piece was exactly one third of the total length. I created a scale model and tested the foldability, which seemed to be good. Then I made a full-sized Styrofoam prototype and fiber glassed it as a one-piece non-folding model. It worked really well and the fins hung down from the sides of the tail and kept it going very straight.

Origami Surf Adventure in Tofino

The one-piece paddleboard worked and was ready for the surf. I was comfortable in how it tested and worked as a one-piece paddleboard. On one of the test trips I wanted to see if I could paddle it through the

surf although it was really intended for calm water because that is what 99 percent of the customers would do with it. I packed my prototype into the car and went up to the coast of Canada at Tofino. It only takes 6 hours to get there, which is a bit longer than going to the Washington coast, but I have a longtime friend there, Louis Rouleau, whom I was overdue to visit. Louis flew small planes in and out of the other remote part of the Canadian coast where I used to live. He always had many interesting stories.

Tofino is near the western end of the Trans-Canada Highway and the only place one can actually drive to open ocean surfing beaches on the west coast of Canada. For Canadians, this is their equivalent of southern California or their Malibu, with all the surf culture but with a polite Canadian style. An, "I'm sorry I just cut you off on that wave," sort of thing. There are tons of places that rent surfboards, so anyone can have a go and try it. There is even a place called "Surf Sisters," catering to girls of any age. Whale watching and fishing are other hot activities and in the winter they people come out to do "storm watching." After growing up on the open ocean, I longed for the beach and the surf, even if it was the middle of winter. I couldn't wait to get in the real Pacific Ocean with the waves.

Even though it was New Year's Day, my dry suit worked well. Aside from a little sweat inside, I was warm and dry. I am not that great of a stand-up surfer, but I found the board to be very stable and after some trial and error I caught some smaller waves. At one point the board rolled over in a funny way that caught the side of my left foot. I kept surfing even though I could now feel my foot felt tweaked. It was a little sore as I carried the board out and up the long beach to the car. That night my foot felt ok but not great. The next day I knew something was wrong because I could hardly walk on it. Pressing in the clutch was difficult in the VW. I barely made it home.

I thought if I stretched my foot out it would feel better. The swelling started to go down but there was still pain and a black line all around the bottom part of the sole of my foot. After a week it still wasn't getting better so I went into a walk-up clinic. I never go to the hospital or see a doctor for anything so I didn't know how to handle it but thought if I wasn't careful it would cost thousands. I had a $2000 deductible on my insurance, so I planned to pay for everything. After a few X-rays, I learned that the outer bone on my left foot was broken. My first broken bone in my whole life.

They sent me to a foot specialist who said that if it didn't set in six weeks, they might have to re-break it or operate, which would take six months to recover from. Then they tried to sell me an inflatable air cast. I asked how much for the air cast? They said they could give me a discount price of $130. I said I would get back with them later.

On the way home, I went to the Goodwill store and found a whole row of inflatable casts for $7 each. It was Discount Tuesday so I would pay only $4.19. Sold! Watersports testing can be hazardous to one's health.

After the surf trip, I cut the board into three pieces and installed a hinge and the buckles to test that. I had plenty of time to hobble around and felt trapped for the next two months as I let my foot heal. Cutting the board worked well and it was really nice to put the folded paddleboard in the back of my little VW Passat wagon to go paddling. The tricky part of this whole venture was that the final folded configuration had to fit the UPS or FedEx sizing to go as regular sized packaging. The formula for that was combined circumference added to the length measurement. All together it had to be 130 inches.

False Assumptions I Made with the Origami

My whole goal with this project was to crowd fund the Origami, have it made, and market it over the Internet. I got some help from a person who did marketing in our area and wasn't young but was sharp. He had never done anything with Kickstarter (the crowd funding website), but knew how to put together a video. He also required $1500 a month to do everything and a percentage of sales that didn't go on forever and that I could cancel out on if I wanted to. I said I would give it two months because I didn't want to start pouring money down a bottomless pit. I had done that before.

We tried to get on Kickstarter, but they simply rejected us with no explanation and no phone number to call for more information. I felt rejected. At least it didn't take long to find out whether or not that route would work.

Trying Our Own Crowd funding

We did our own www.origamipaddler.com website and video to try to do our own crowd funded campaign. After two months we'd had no response. I thought, let's go for another month. Still nothing. I told the marketer that I couldn't afford to go any further, so we ended our relationship amicably. I kept everything up on the site, but didn't expect anything to happen. Then in the fourth month, the video got picked up by Gizmag, which is like an online Popular Mechanics site that has a large following. In two weeks, I sold 30 boards and had just over $20,000. This was shy of our goal to have enough for the molds and the first run. I still had to build the patterns that the molds would be made from. I had done this before but knew it was a lot of work.

I had a bit of indecision about going forward underfunded, but figured when we got the boards done, I wouldn't have to sell many to create some cash flow. Finally, in the fall, we had the molds and made some boards. I still wasn't completely sure that making the Origamis out of polyethylene would feel right in the water. I knew it would be strong. The first ones that came out were disappointing but we added more plastic and the boards got strong enough but were not light. They were still better than putting a long board on top of the car. The sales had fallen off because our marketing fire had gone out while I made the first run of boards.

THIRTY-EIGHT

GETTING THE ORIGAMI PADDLER INTO AMAZON

"No matter which way you paddle,
it is always uphill and against the current."

I wanted to get the Origami up for sale on Amazon. Over the next year, I tried to get people to market the product but found that it took a lot of different skills to reach people over the Internet. I had met someone who helped people get going on the Amazon Vendor account, which you must set up if you want Amazon to actually buy and stock your product. Even with the help, it was extremely difficult. I don't know how Amazon makes any money. The person from Amazon who handled our account took months to get back with us, but we finally got the OK to have them sell our product. It was now late fall and we had missed the season. The percentage that they took combined with the extra cut that the person helping us get on to Amazon was over 50%, and Amazon would take three months to pay, and they wanted money for fees before they paid us. Also we had to pay Larry Schonemacher to build the boards in 30 days, so we would have to come up with money to pay the manufacturer before we got paid.

Tracy really wanted to keep her hands clean of my ventures, but she was the only person that could make this happen. I hired some really smart people to try to deal with Amazon, and it was too much for them. We reasoned that if we kept our price at the same as on Amazon, we could pull in a few direct sales.

Our original goals for the Origami were to be crowd funded and get on Amazon. We eventually got on Amazon. Amazon could set the price and they set it low to get sales started. We only made between $100 and $200 on each board, which didn't seem worth it because we had to come up with money to pay Larry to mold the boards for us. Having Amazon set the price so low meant that we couldn't even make much if we tried to sell them on our own site. We had sold some of them to dealers without a storefront, guys that just sold them out of their garage. This can work beautifully if the dealer takes people out on the water, which is not something that many storefront dealers do. These "garage dealers" could not compete against Amazon pricing because the boards were sold online for less than these dealers paid for the boards. Instead of being our salvation, Amazon pricing was making life difficult.

Reviews on the Internet can be harsh. We had a few hinges break, not from use but from the UPS delivery. The hinges held up fine for the customers. I wanted to have hand holds in the shipping boxes because they were an awkward size and hard to hold on to. UPS said not to put any holes in the box but I knew that bicycle boxes always had them. The first boxes went out without the holes, and arrived with broken hinges. The hinges were made for hatches and I couldn't break them when I used them. I think only one of our customers ever broke them, but UPS managed to.

Moving from Idea to Reality with More Efficiency

In some ways, moving from idea to reality is more important than the art that originally inspired me to create watercraft in the first place. Sometimes I say that kayaks are kinetic sculptures, or that they are prosthetic devices for the aquatically challenged. They are both those things, as well as being art you can use. It is one challenge to take an idea and transform it into reality whether anyone cares about it or not, like a painting in an art gallery. My challenge is always to take my idea and translate it into an experience for a billion people. It's much more challenging than creating static art.

What is My Best Role to Play in the Future?

After I had run the gamut from idea to reality once and somehow made it through to the other side, how would I do it again? Why would I even want to do it again? What would I do differently? I still really struggle with this because now I come at this issue from a different perspective.

Let Family In or Keep Them Out?

I struggle with whether or not to involve family members in my business ventures. In one sense, who could be closer to understanding what is going on in the business than a family member? On the other hand, how could you ever fire a close family member? When a company is for sale, the very people that made the company what it is are also what can kill a sale. I have been told that new owners of a company don't like to deal with a fraternity of a family that wants to run the company their way. The new owners don't share the same passion for having family members succeed in spite of the company.

If your family member is part of your business, keep your role and theirs separate. Try not to share all the details of how risky one deal is over another. It is very difficult for me to maintain these boundaries because I am always depending on someone to bounce ideas off of. I have tried making someone's compensation dependent on what I earn, say in something like consulting. It's great if the other person looks at things differently than I do.

A healthy tension can be beneficial. The relationship is like a kite and a string. The kite wants to soar but will eventually vanish or fall if it is not securely grounded with the string.

Making Good Agreements

The key to family or other business relationships are good agreements. The word agreement to me sounds better than contract because it suggests that it is mutually beneficial. Agreements don't have to be an inch thick with boilerplate verbiage that requires a lawyer to interpret. An agreement can be as simple as you get 1/3rd and I get 1/3rd and the other third goes into operating expenses. Be precise about what the 1/3rd consists of. Be precise about who decides what and when. What are the minimum expectations? Make sure all the responsibilities are covered by someone who has the authority to do the specified job. Remember everything is measurable, but impartial measurement may take a third party. Write it all out. Then have a simple exit strategy that everybody agrees to at the beginning. Don't wait till the end to do that, because then it usually doesn't go well.

Working with Others

I have learned that I do not work well by myself. I need to have someone else to bounce ideas off of. For many others, and me the creative process is like a conversation. I find it much more satisfying to work with others, because the process becomes a celebration with a team. Sometimes I find if I talk something through with another person, then suddenly things start making more sense. When I explain things, I understand them better myself. I think this may be a key part of why I was not as effective as I could have been on some of the projects I worked on.

Plan for a Successful Business

Start with a plan. This will save you a lot of time in the long run. Planning doesn't mean that you lose your drive and passion for what you are doing, but refines the direction you are headed in so you will get there quicker via a more direct route. Planning together is a great way to get everyone in the organization all on the same page.

Creating a Branding Statement

Write a branding statement. This is the DNA of what you're doing and can even be a statement for what you stand for and what you are trying to accomplish. This is what you should put on your business card or tell the person you just met in the elevator. Keep it short. Your branding statement should answer the following questions: (1) What do you do, (2) Why do you do it, (3) Who do you do it for, and (4) How is it better.

Start by writing many sentences on each of these four questions, at least a full page on each. Then perfect and keep only one sentence per question. This can and should take hours. After that, reduce each sentence to about two words so you have about an eight-word statement that answers all four questions. It can be reworked but shouldn't be ever changing, because then it can appear to people that you don't really know what you are doing. I did this exercise all day and came up with a four-word branding statement: "Small boats, big dreams." A longer version was "We build small boats for your big dreams."

THIRTY-NINE

SETTING GOALS

"If you fail to set goals and plan for them it can turn into a plan to fail while getting lost at the same time."

In my first business, Ocean Kayak, I kept my goals in my head and didn't share them and it took me a long time to achieve them. Run your long or short-term goals through the test below to see if your goals are really realistic. This is a good exercise if your spouse is not working in the business but does have an understanding of what the bottom line is. Within your company, it keeps everyone aware of where the organization is. Make sure the goal is relevant for everyone working towards it. Everyone has to own it. The first letters spell SMART. I never knew how important this exercise was until I wrote down my goals. Someone found that when goals were spoken, the chance of the goals becoming real went up to 30%. If it was written down, the chance of success went up to 60%, and if they were written and worked into a daily plan, the chance went from 60% to 100%. Now, when I decide to do something with well-defined goals, I get to the finish line much faster. Your goals must be: (1) Specific, (2) Measurable, (3) Achievable, (4) Relevant, and (5) Timely.

Remember that everything is measurable, although that may require input from a third party. Relevant means everyone is on board with this goal and agrees that it should happen and is excited about it. The classic goal in the 1960s, as stated by John F. Kennedy, was "a man on the moon by the end of this decade." This simple goal was one that everyone knew and embraced and may be one of the major reasons it actually happened.

Sticky Ideas

Some of my ideas stuck (meaning they are still memorable and successful) and some didn't. I now have some clues as to which ones may have a better chance in the future. Someone said we get 5000 messages a day, especially if you watch much TV. We only remember about three and why is that? Someone did a study and discovered that the ideas that did stick had the elements shown below. These are generally a little more emotional than the SMART goals above. To be "sticky," an idea must be: (1) Simple, (2) Unexpected, (3) Credible, (4) Concrete, (5) Emotional, and (6) Story.

You might note that the first letters of all these characteristics spell SUCCES. The "emotional story" aspect really fascinated me but when I look at a news story that gets people talking, it usually has these elements. The Simple and Unexpected grabs your attention, and the Emotional Story hooks you.

These Sticky Ideas are great for promotions and fundraising on sites like Kickstarter. If you look through the successful crowd funded campaigns, many of them have these elements. These days I don't waste time having a campaign fail because I forgot to look at it through a filter like this before I start. A much higher percentage of my campaigns are successful now.

Consulting with Packages and Deliverables

Is consulting the right thing to do after you sell your company? In some ways, consulting is heaven because you get to suggest all the cool ideas to people that are like grandkids in that they want to believe anything and will actually pay you for advice, sometimes in advance. Many of the consultants that I have used over the years admit that they are really not that good at managing companies but they love certain aspects of the business or are good at just getting things done. At first for me consulting was just too fun. When I first started consulting I didn't know how to stop just talking to the person and start charging. I could just sit around talking boats for the next six years. I finally had to set a limit on how much "casual conversation" I would have before asking for money. Don't get me wrong, I loved every minute of the consulting work but had other things to do if I wasn't getting paid.

I decided to give the potential clients one hour of "free" time where I would describe what I could do for them and why it is valuable. If the one-hour turned into two, I usually let that slip by, but no more. I would agree to give them "deliverables," which is a specific definable amount of information for a price. The price was for ten hours at between $100 and $200 per hour. For small boats, the deliverable was to tell them the weight and the price of the finished product made from either vacuum-formed plastic or rotomolded plastic.

The other dollar figure I would give them is the approximate price to set up production, which mainly centered on the mold cost. With this information, they could either stop and keep their regular day job or do what it would take to forge ahead. If they came up with a pricing structure, then they could figure out how much they could make. If they did a crowd funded campaign, they could have their first customers before they bought their mold. If they had a good business plan, they could figure out how many boats it would take to break even and make that their goal for the campaign. Crowd financing is great because after you give them the boats, usually at a discount, your funding source, the customer, is not a partner you have to keep happy.

If there were time I would carve my consulting clients a scale model that they could hold in their hands. I would answer any questions about what I knew or had seen as far as successful methods of getting their product on the market. For me, this was the fun part. It felt like starting a company every few months with the money up front but no headaches or equity.

For me, after discussing the initial plan, goals, and budget, the next step is making a prototype of the new boat. More than half of my clients want to go ahead and have a full-size model and other work done to get into production. The first step is the working prototype. These prototypes are relatively inexpensive and can be used to make videos that show the new boat in action, to demonstrate to people in a crowd funded situation that the product will really works. With some crowd-funded campaigns, people try to raise money from computer simulations of boat designs. Personally, I would not put money down on only a computer simulation, no matter what the discount because it just isn't real.

Showing a full-size prototype of a kayak is a good proof of concept. I made prototypes in my small shop that didn't have much overhead and with labor that was not full time. It's hard to have a steady flow of work doing R&D. Everyone either doesn't want to pay for any work, or they want the work yesterday. I have a full-size CNC machine that we can make foam prototypes on.

We did the prototype and first mold work for NuCanoe, Diablo Paddlesports, and KC Kayaks as well as the original Top Dog Paddleboard, Lifetime paddleboard, and a new powered boat like a paddleboard called the Tiburon. While working with Diablo, we wanted to make the showroom boat to hit the same season we were in so we worked from a little foam model that I showed over Skype on two laptop computers to the bosses in Texas. The scale model was only 1/6th scale or 2 inches to a foot on the small model. A one-foot-tall wood mannequin I got from Ikea was my scale test paddler. The Texans liked it so we put the shape on CAD and carved out full-size molds. The material the boats were to be made from was ABS vacuum-formed parts. The first carved-out wood molds worked for the halves for the first 12 boats. After that the wood starts to disintegrate, so fiberglass molds are made. The halves from the wood molds are assembled and tested. The bad news for this method of construction is that the materials are more expensive and there is more labor required because they have to be put together, resulting in a boat that retails from between $1,000 and $2,000, compared to rotomolding where the molds are $40,000 but the boats retail for $500 to $1,000. The good news with the vacuum forming is that the boats are super shiny and much stiffer and about 30% lighter. The molds are also much cheaper at around $10,000 apiece.

FORTY

DONATE YOUR TIME TO A WORTHWHILE CAUSE

"There are those that make things happen, those that watch things happen and those that wonder what happened."

If you sold your company for a lot of money, then maybe it would be more enjoyable to donate your time rather than charge for it. If you aren't getting paid, it may be a lot easier to quit. I suppose one might not really consider this consulting, but it is close. I have done consulting for nonprofit organizations, and it is really fun.

I have even done project management consulting and what surprised me is that I could do it as well for someone else as I could do for my own business. Somehow, answering to someone else, and especially using their money, took all the pressure off me so I could do my part. A consultant plays a smaller but still very important part and maybe the consultant doesn't get burned out like a day-to-day business owner can. Consulting can carry the excitement without the hassle of day-to-day business life.

Serving on a Board of Directors

Serving on a board can also give you the feeling of contributing along with the freedom from the day-to-day grind. Ideally, serving on the board of a company means that you are a part of the planning committee that sets the direction and holds the company leader accountable for the goals that were already set earlier by that board. The leader of the organization's sole purpose is to carry out those specific goals. Being a member of this team is also satisfying because it's nice to be around like-minded people. Some charity boards don't pay and some for profitable businesses pay well. I found that I was on some boards that didn't do any planning, or did very little. They were controlled by the company or organization. Some of them were very close-knit family type operations that had their way of running things and the board had to fit into that mold.

Sometimes the main function of the board is to attract rich associates and convince them to supply donations. I was on a board once that was for a great private school. My contribution to the board was this idea: for different levels of contribution by people in the community, the school could offer contributors (and only if they chose that option) a certain level of interaction or involvement. For example, a big contributor could get a front row seat to speak with the students or the staff. This particular school took a trip to Cuba, which was very adventurous considering that the U.S. didn't at that time have diplomatic relations with that country. What a learning experience. What if the donor earned some level of involvement on that trip? Maybe he or she or they could even go on the trip? It was very worthwhile to be a part of an organization that was making a difference. As you can see, being on a board can be interesting, amusing, entertaining, and rewarding.

Redefining Success

What is success anyway? How much is enough? Why do we do it and what do we get out of it? Are we here just to see who can make the most amount of money or is success measured in some other value. Is it that we are out to change the world? Are we trying to satisfy something we wanted as a child and didn't get? Then later in life we have this  desire that comes out of nowhere to create this business or accomplish something? How come it can seem like filling a bottomless pit? What makes us want to do all of this?

For me, I no longer look for satisfaction in what I call empire building. I delight in very simple things that work. I still love to solve puzzles. This just happened the other day with the Origami Paddler. A woman with a convertible wanted to get an Origami Paddler, but it didn't quite fit in her car. When I tried to change the Origami for this person, I decided to make a special one for her out of a new material. I wouldn't have done that if I hadn't been asked in the first place. We'll see how it turns out but I wouldn't have tried it if she hadn't had the need. Solving an individual challenge is so different from building a product for a large company with mindless test marketing and no face-to-face conversations. Sometimes it's that one customer that makes the difference in getting the ball rolling.

Reflections

After selling Ocean Kayak, it was easy to feel like all the intensity of that moment was gone. What did life mean anymore? There was no group or tribe to both hassle me and keep me alive. On the other hand, there was a lot less stress and it was easier to focus on the smaller things in life. Now the moment is in satisfying that one customer you will include in your book!

All of my Dreamer, Hunter, Craftsman, and Visionary energies had to take a forced vacation for a while, and not all of those personas were ready for that. You should think about this even before you start a company. Actually, the best time to create your exit strategy is before starting the challenge. You may not want to sell your company, but instead pass it on to your kids. This works if they don't fight or if you make arrangements so that infighting doesn't happen. The future success depends on whether there is a passion there to continue the business. If this does look like your future, condition yourself to let it happen and be able to leave.

Working on a board can be a great way of providing direction without doing much day-to-day work, if you get on a properly run board. This can also be very satisfying with nonprofits, because your efforts can really affect people's lives; not just make profits.

They say that after a big breakup, it may be good to not jump right into another big relationship. The same may be true for getting into another big company. If you do go back into business, choose the people you work with carefully. Working alone may not be satisfying, or may be more satisfying. I am a people person and really like to work with the right people.

It's not about the money. It's about finding a meaningful place in the world.

CONCLUSION . . .

"The universe is really very simple

but the explanation can be a bit more complicated."

You may be one of those people who read the conclusion first. If you are, you may be surprised to hear that this is not a manual about how to hang out on the beach and make millions of dollars while drinking beer. Well, maybe parts of it are, but there is a little more to it than that.

This book is about how I was able to turn a life dominated by fears, the first being the fear of water, into a life of joy of being on the water. I still slip into doing things out of fear, or because "I have to."

For me, there is hardly a greater feeling than merging fantastic dreams and reality into the present moment that takes your breath away. I have been fortunate to make this happen in my life. How did this come to pass?

All my life I struggled with fears fighting my passions, with a little ADD (Attention Deficit Disorder) thrown in to mix things up even more. Writing this book is a way of forcing myself to understand my journey, with you, the reader, as the witness. Fear is how I felt in reaction to the big world when I was younger. Passion is what I get from overcoming that fear.

Thom Hartmann writes about ADD and ADHD (in this book, I use ADD for both) as a blessing, not a curse. In his book, The Edison Gene: ADHD and the Gift of the Hunter Child, he makes a good case for ADD being a specific gene that made us what we are as humans. There is a lot of evidence that many of the great innovators had ADD behavior. In Hartman's other book, Beyond ADD: Hunting for Reasons in the Past and in the Present, he compares ADD behavior to that of a hunter and more focused behavior as that of a farmer. He argues that we are living in a more agrarian world now where the hunter doesn't fit in.

I have made reference to this hunter versus farmer way of looking at my life and my behaviors. I have tried to share my strategies for dealing with a hunter mentality in growing up because sometimes hunters don't fit in at first. This individuality can create innovation: someone who doesn't fit the common mold can come up with something completely new and novel.

The whole dance I had with the ocean was much like the dance I have had with my subconscious mind, which has my past wrapped up in it. The fears I had when going into the big ocean, at a young age, all by myself, were much like confronting my fears of the past that are lurking under the surface of my conscious self. Being on the ocean surface gave me the ability to confront and be literally "on top" of these fears in the smallest of vessels, the kayak.

There are physiological and genetic differences in the spectrum of ADD that can create a different way for the ADD mind to perceive the world. When this is better understood, then relationships may start to make a little more sense and make ideas come into focus.

To explain my ideas in the Reflections sections, I use Carl Jung's archetypes of men: King, Warrior, Lover, and Magician. The Lover, which I refer to in this book as the Dreamer, is the energy of new beginnings, like that of the early morning or springtime. It is the energy of lust and love, the energy of innovation and creative activity.

The Warrior is like the Hunter, it relates to the Hunter–Farmer relationship. For Carl Jung, the Hunter is the energy of action and getting things done, of setting boundaries and cutting clean when necessary. Jung refers to the energy of the Magician as one who can create transformation, like the alchemist who can transform lead to gold. I call the Magician the Craftsman. This energy is that of the person who makes things with his hands.

The King or Queen is also the Visionary. This is the energy of the sovereign who looks after the good of the whole kingdom for both the short and long term, the wise Visionary who can look into the future and visualize something great.

This book is also about growing up in Malibu, living an exciting and fulfilling life with fascinating experiences, enjoying a great career in the paddlesports industry, and meeting some of the great watermen of our time. I hope you have found it interesting.

WORK IN PROGRESS

This book has been a great process for me and it has given me a great insight to see it all in one place. No doubt I will re do it more than once. If you have any suggestions or insights please tell me about them. I will try to spend more time on my social media or email me. tim@timniemier.com

ACKNOWLEDGEMENTS

I would like to acknowledge my parents who were so patient with me, my brother who always loved me in his own crazy way. The many teachers and adults that influenced me when I was growing up. All my family members for their patience and understanding. All the people I have worked for or worked with for their understanding and willingness to try something new or stand up to me when I needed it.

I love the people who surround me in my life right now more than anything. To everyone else who I have either met or not met who have had an influence on who I am, I hope I have had some sort of positive influence on others, even though I am by no means perfect myself. For anyone not included in what I have said here, you know who you are and thank you, thank you, thank you.

Made in the USA
San Bernardino, CA
14 September 2015